© Copyright 2021 - All rights reserved.

You may not reproduce, duplicate or send the contents of this book without direct written permission from the author. You cannot hereby despite any circumstance blame the publisher or hold him or her to legal responsibility for any reparation, compensations, or monetary forfeiture owing to the information included herein, either in a direct or an indirect way.

Legal Notice: This book has copyright protection. You can use the book for personal purpose. You should not sell, use, alter, distribute, quote, take excerpts or paraphrase in part or whole the material contained in this book without obtaining the permission of the author first.

Disclaimer Notice: You must take note that the information in this document is for casual reading and entertainment purposes only. We have made every attempt to provide accurate, up to date and reliable information. We do not express or imply guarantees of any kind. The persons who read admit that the writer is not occupied in giving legal, financial, medical or other advice. We put this book content by sourcing various places.

Please consult a licensed professional before you try any techniques shown in this book. By going through this document, the book lover comes to an agreement that under no situation is the author accountable for any forfeiture, direct or indirect, which they may incur because of the use of material contained in this document, including, but not limited to errors, omissions, or inaccuracies.

A Very Merry Christmas Activity Book

This book belongs to

CONNECT THE DOTS

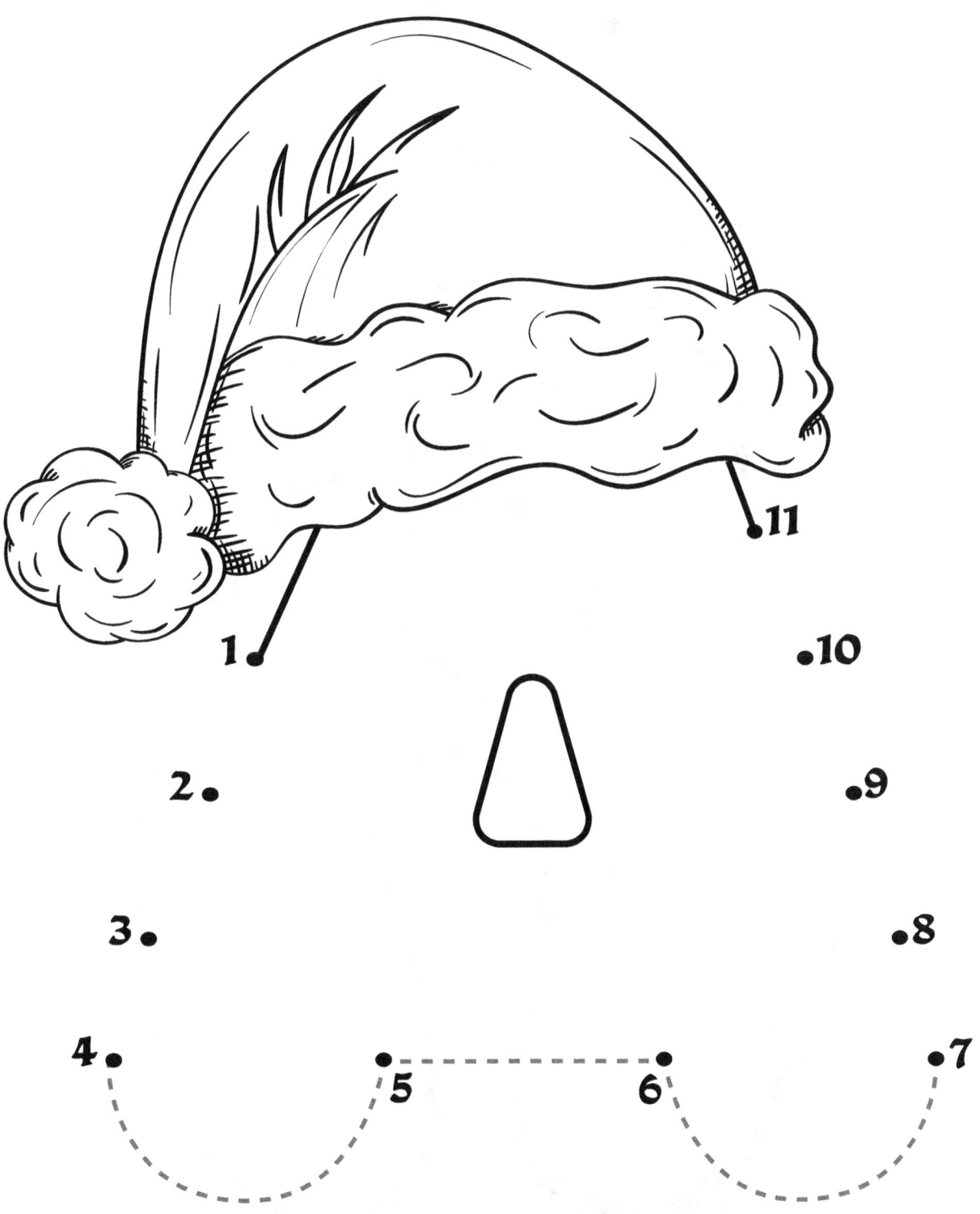

A COLOR IT

A a

CONNECT THE DOTS

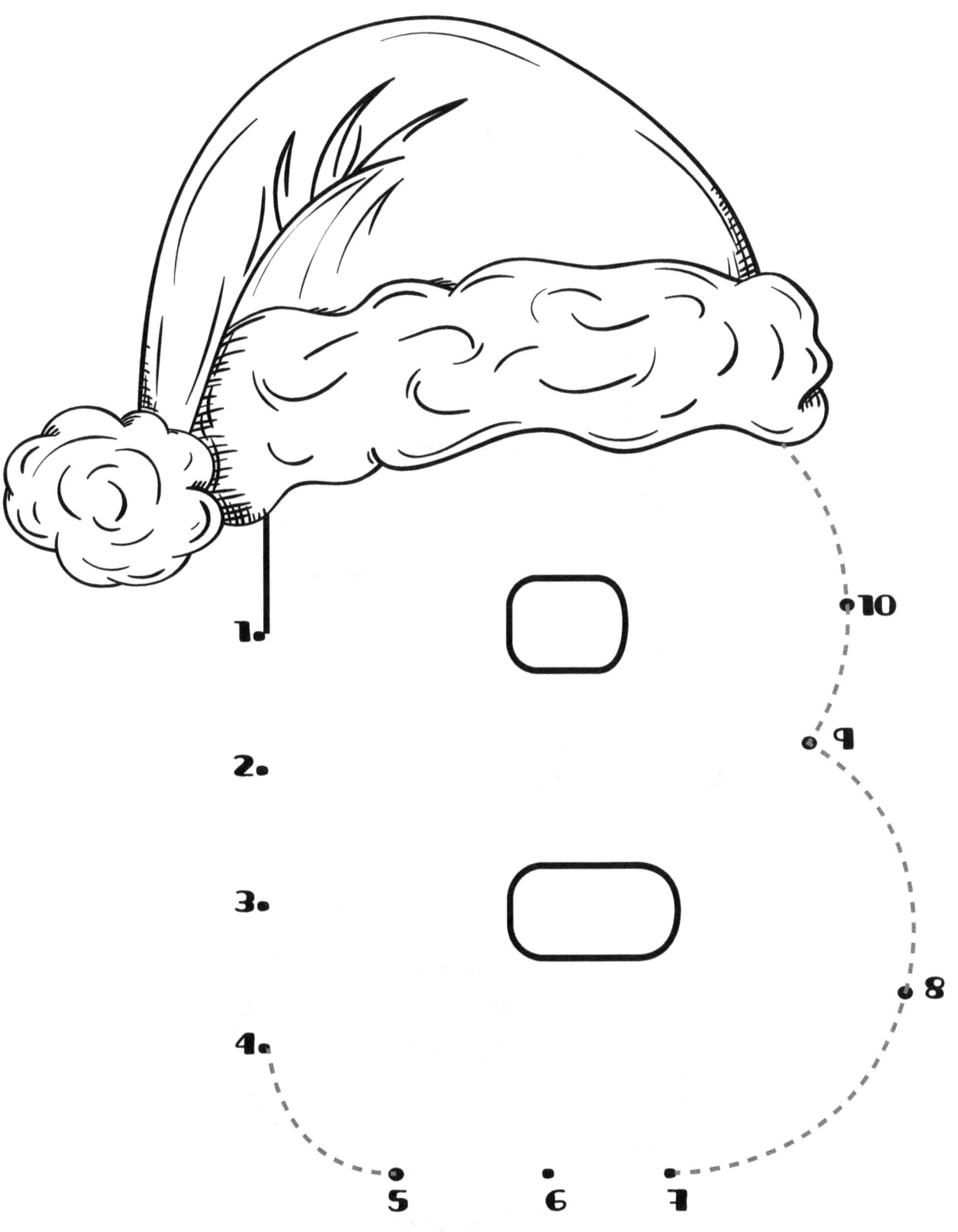

B COLOR IT

B b

CONNECT THE DOTS

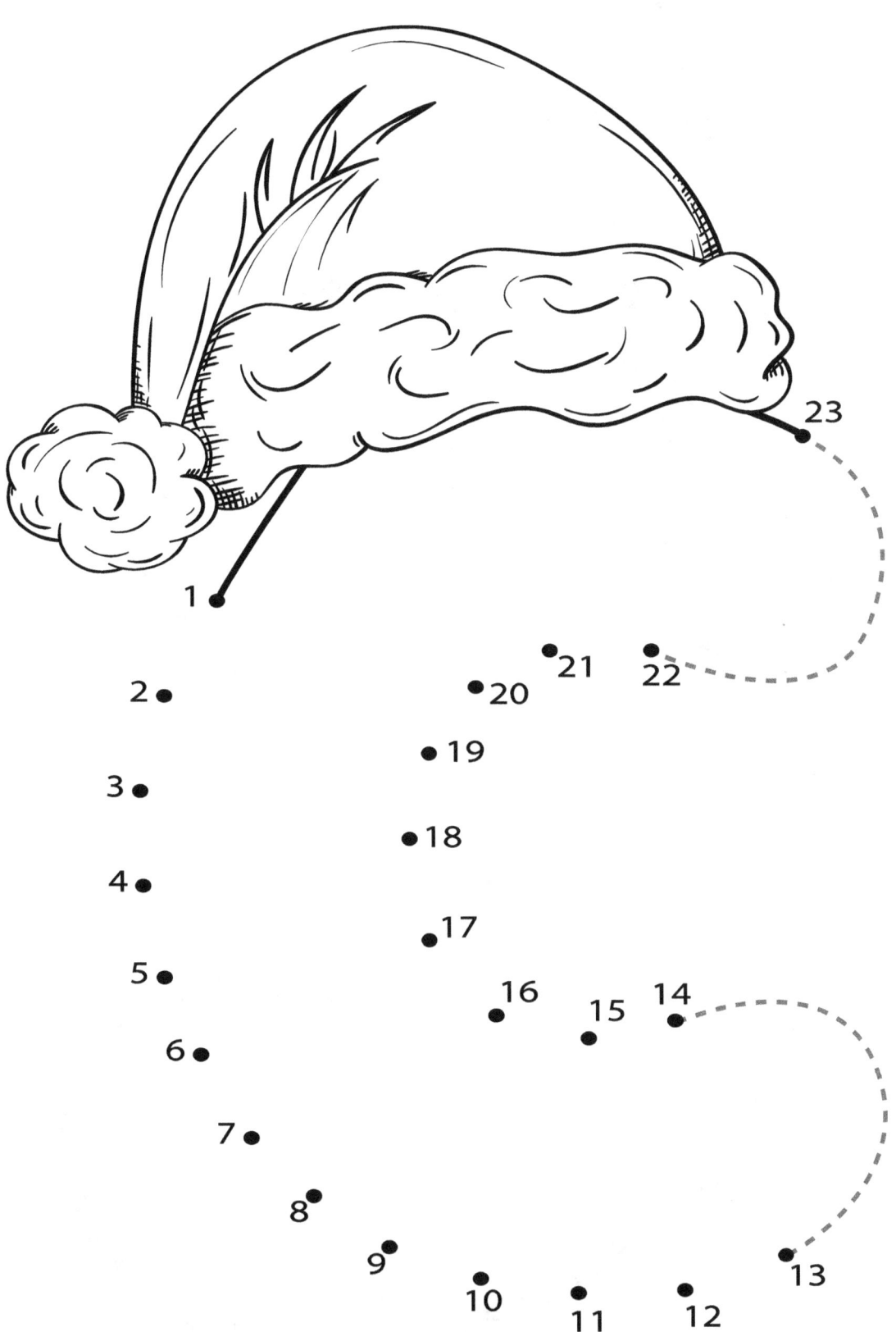

C COLOR IT

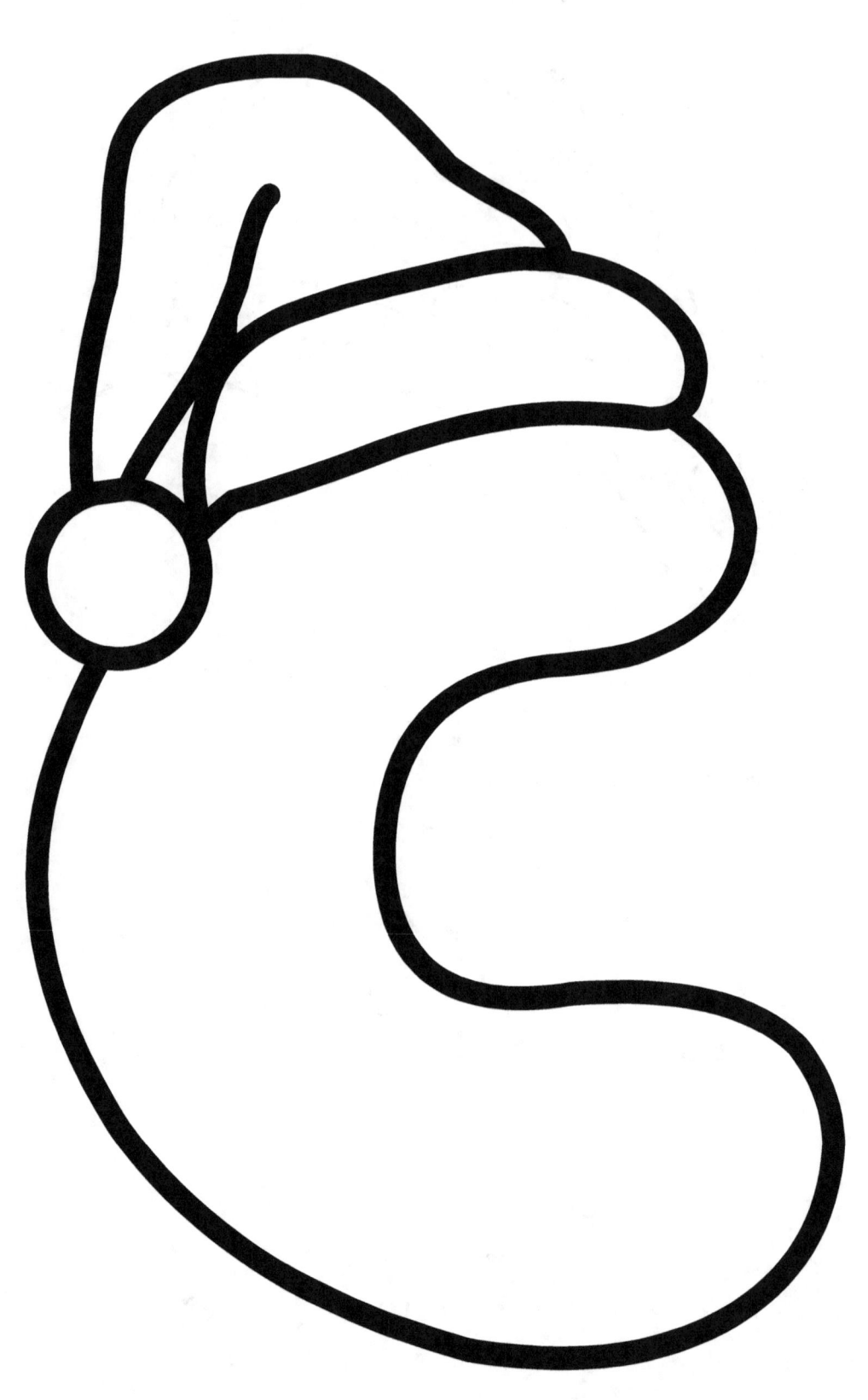

CONNECT THE DOTS

D COLOR IT

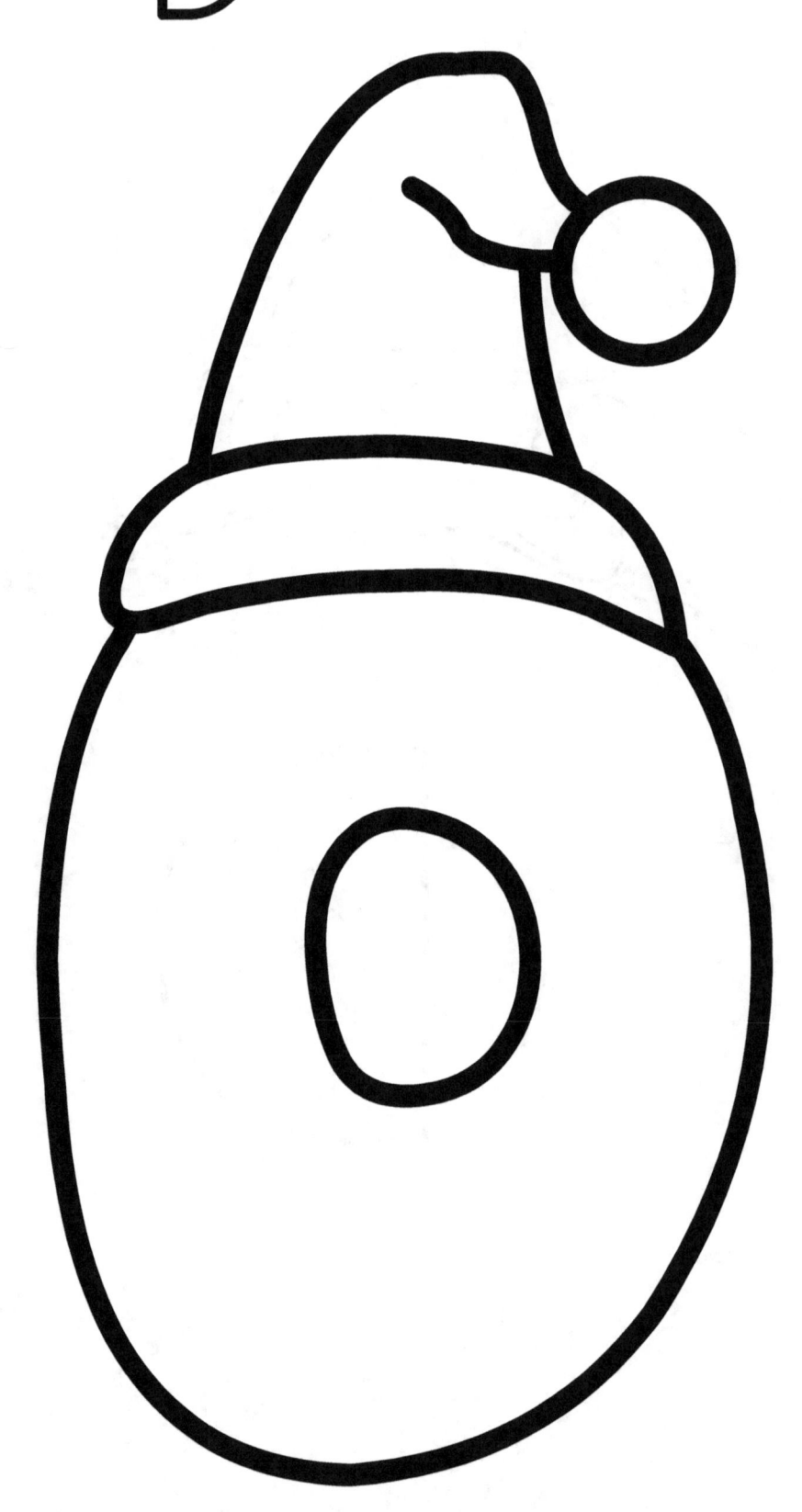

D d

CONNECT THE DOTS

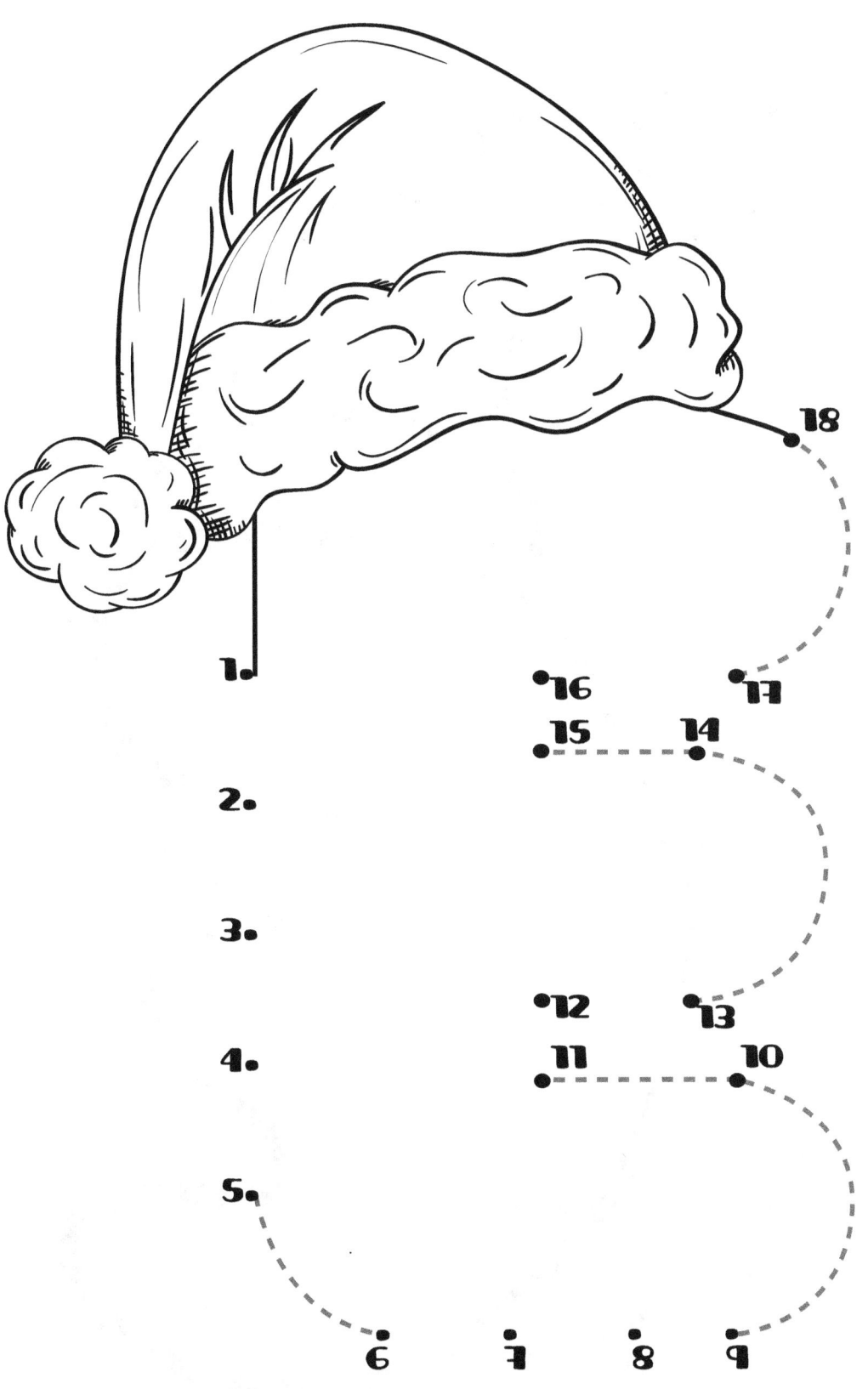

E COLOR IT

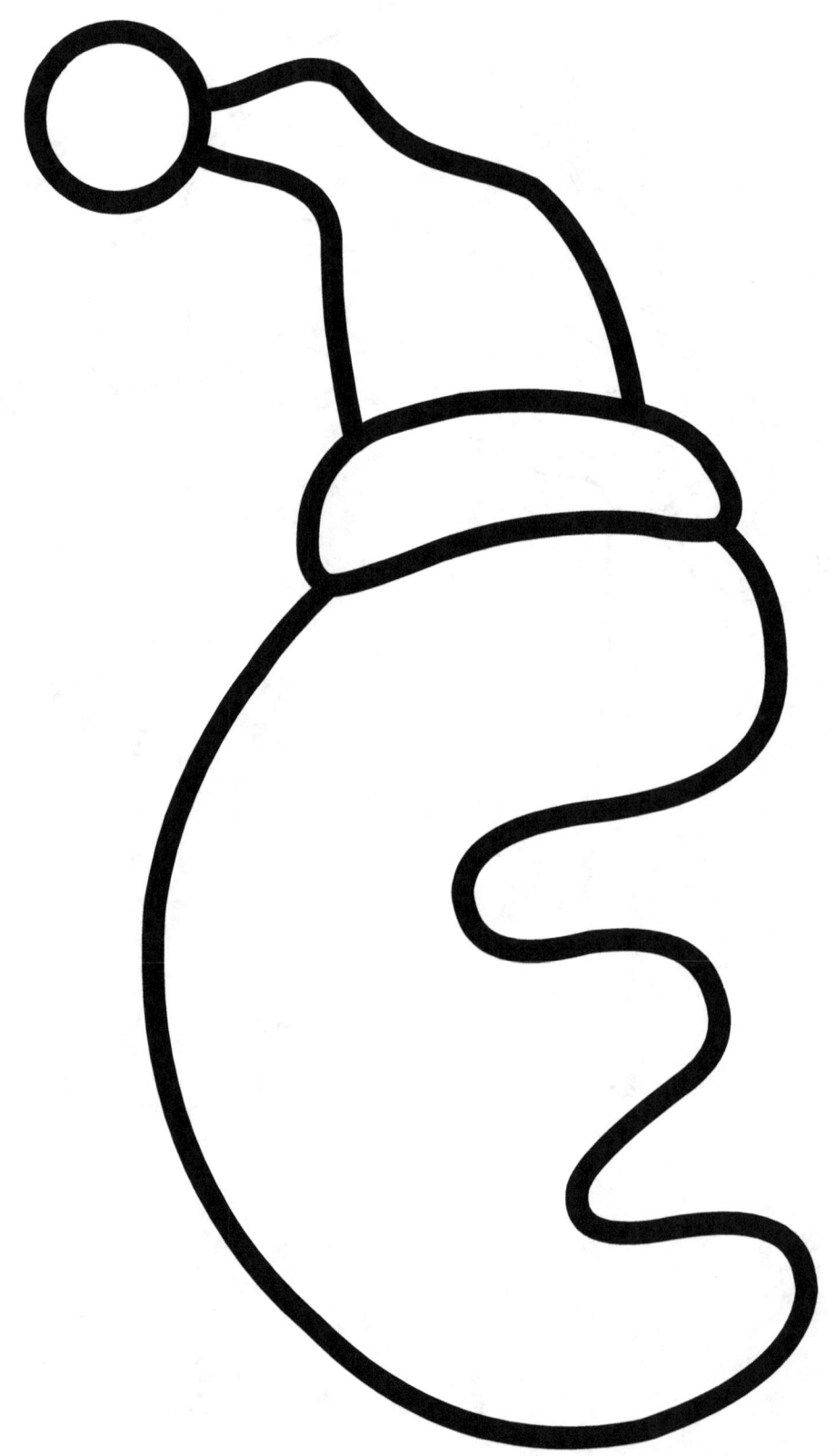

E e

CONNECT THE DOTS

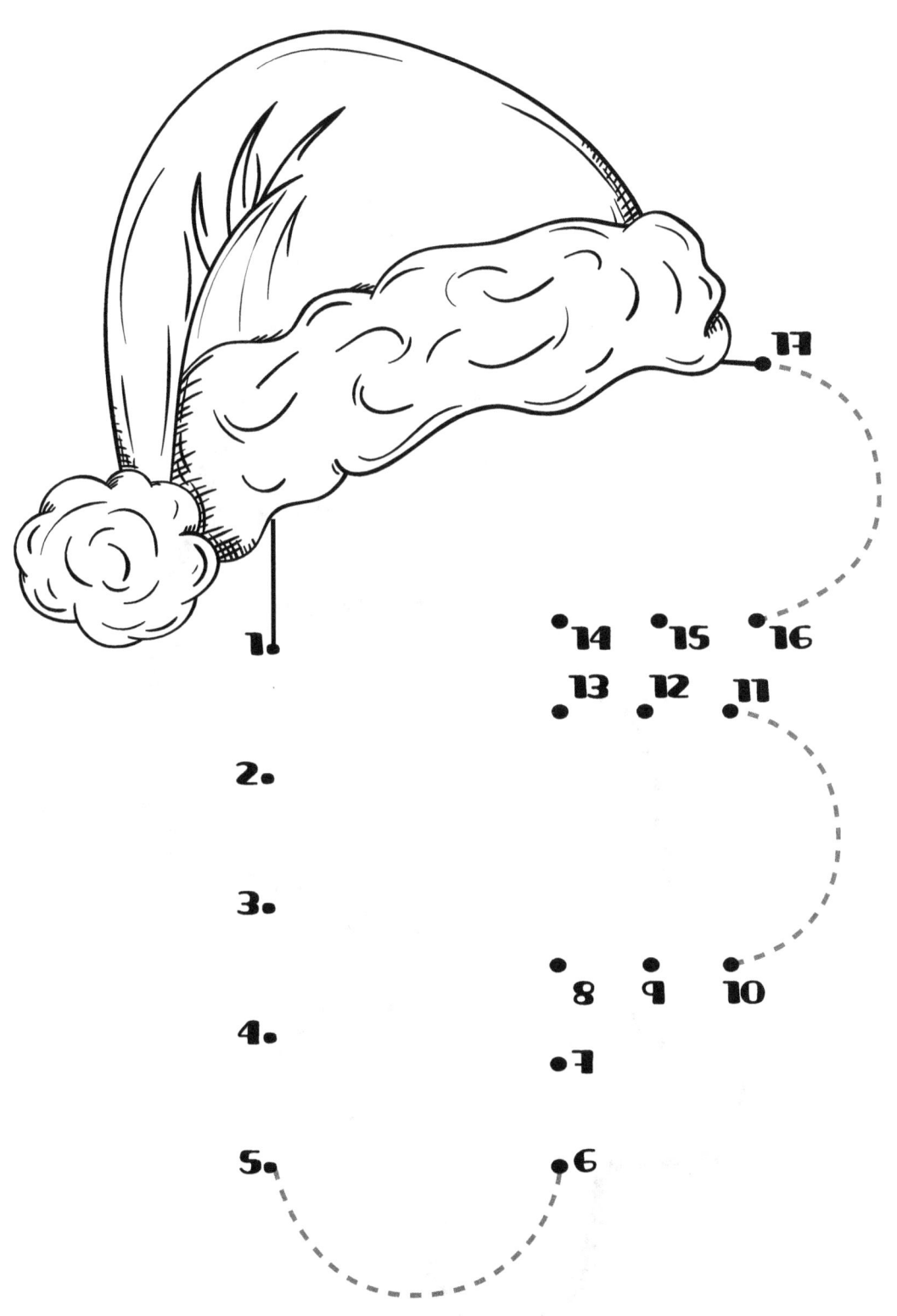

F COLOR IT

CONNECT THE DOTS

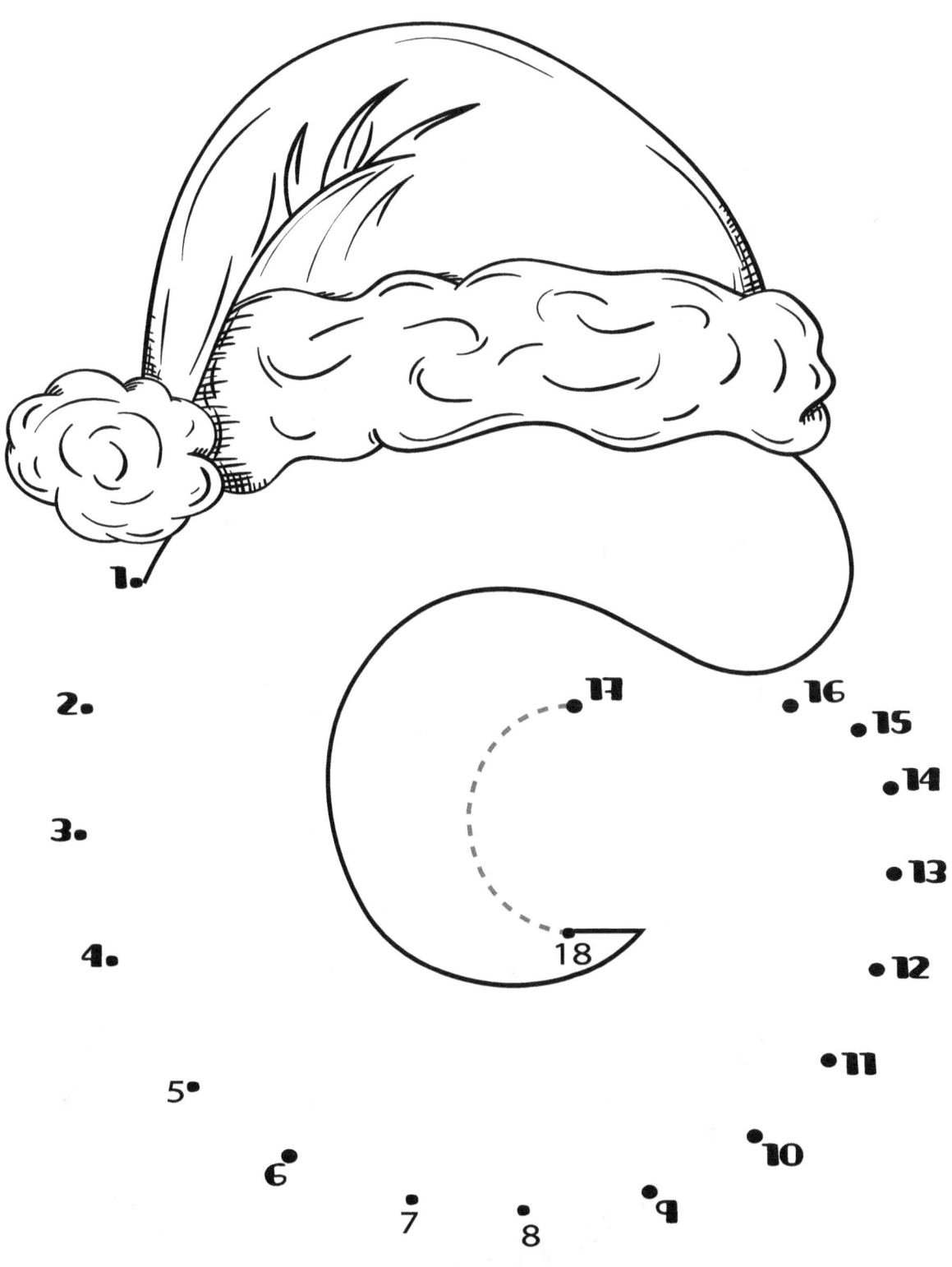

G color it

G g

CONNECT THE DOTS

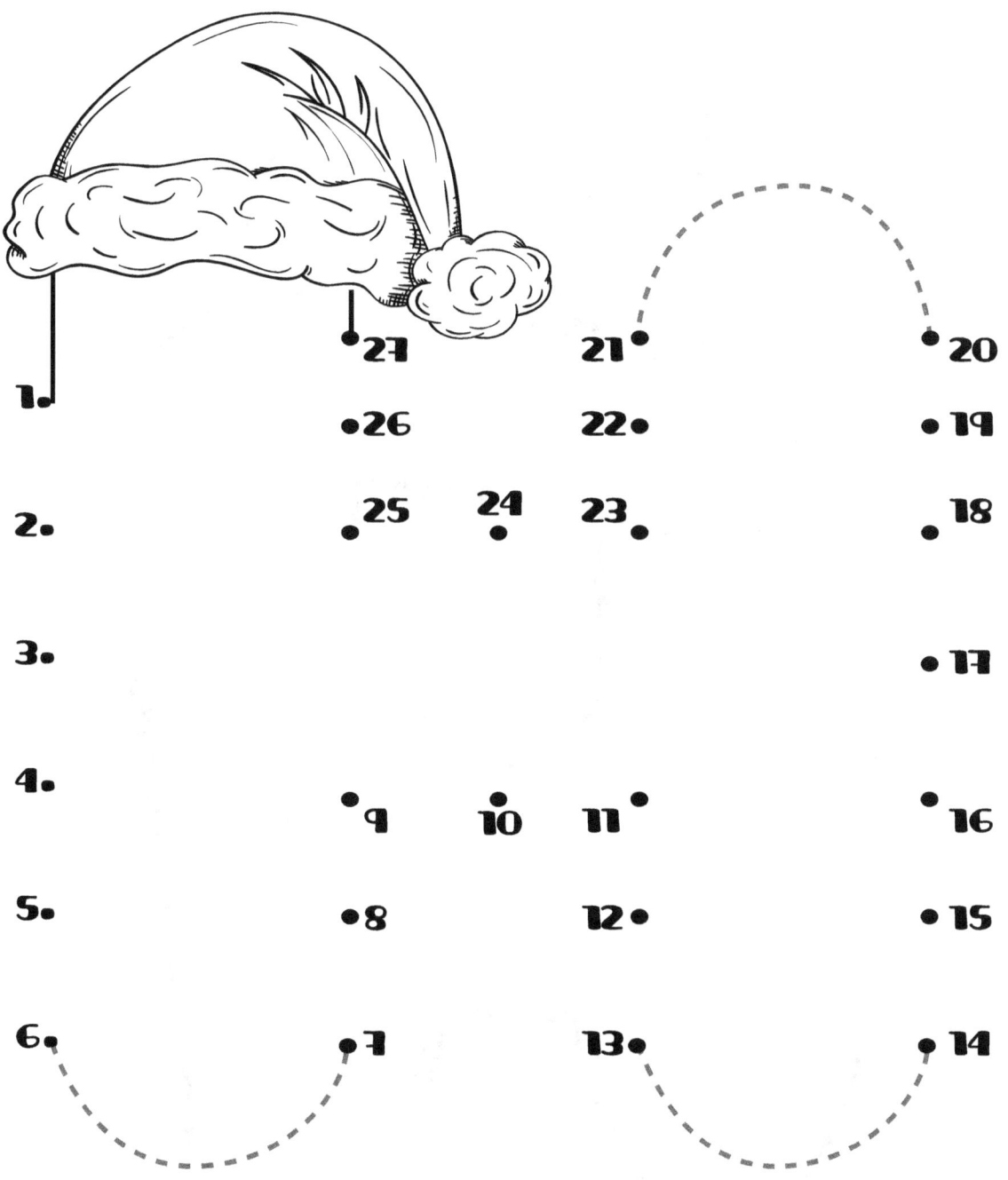

COLOR IT

H h

CONNECT THE DOTS

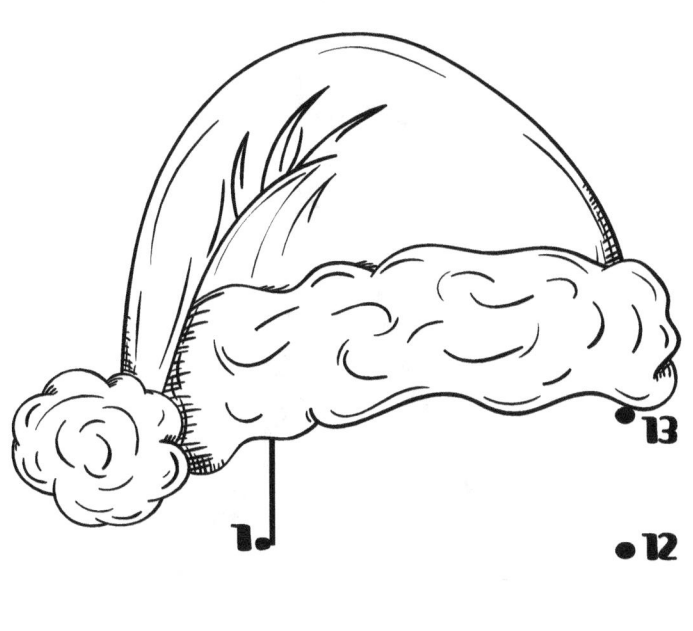

COLOR IT

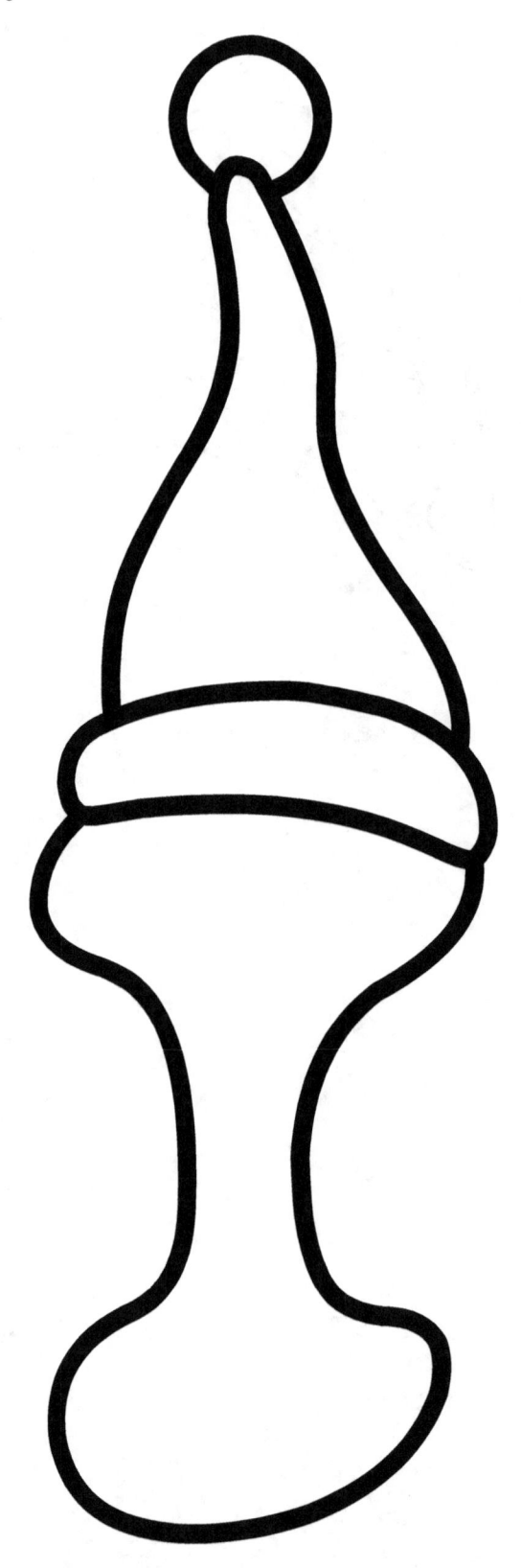

CONNECT THE DOTS

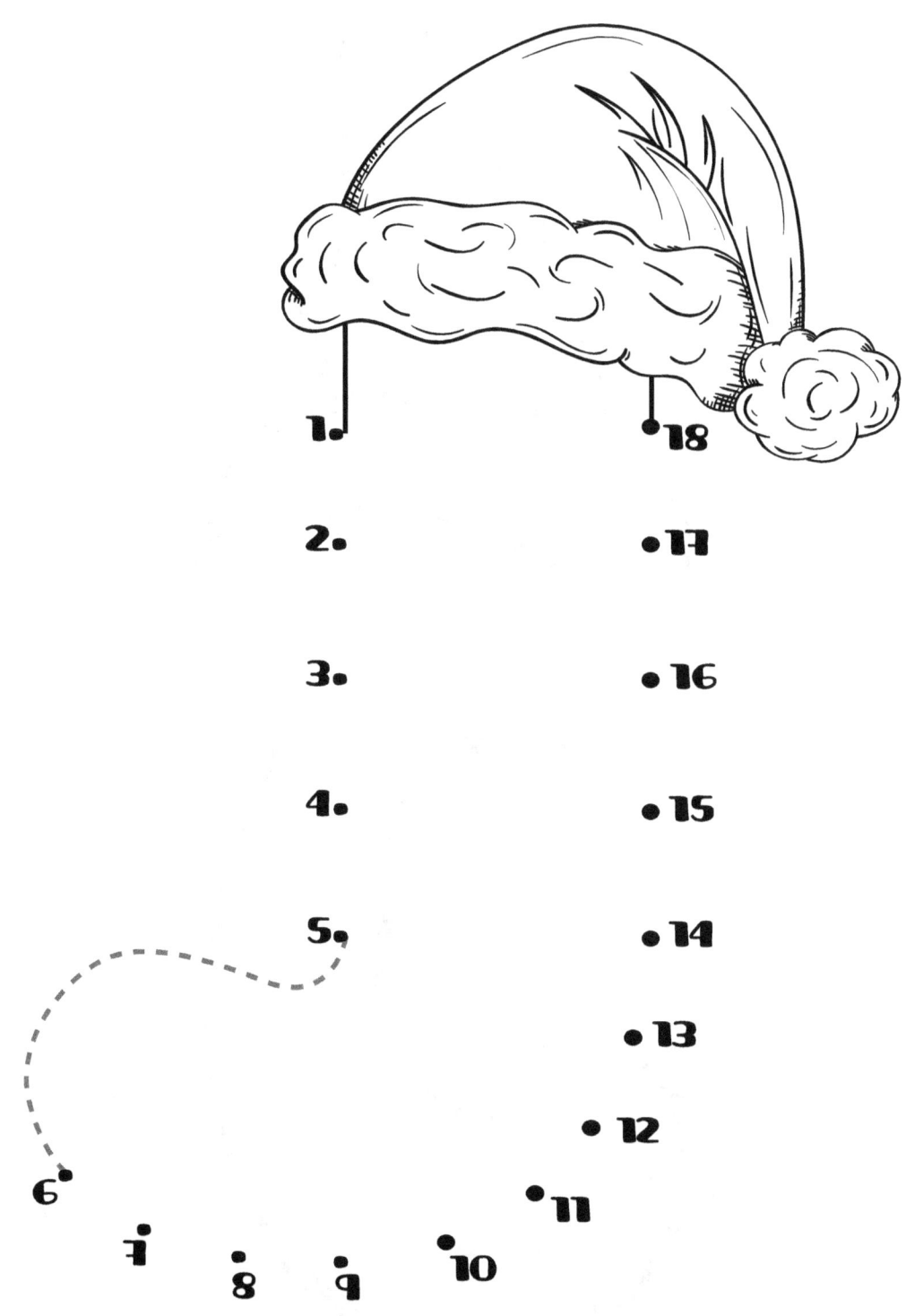

J COLOR IT

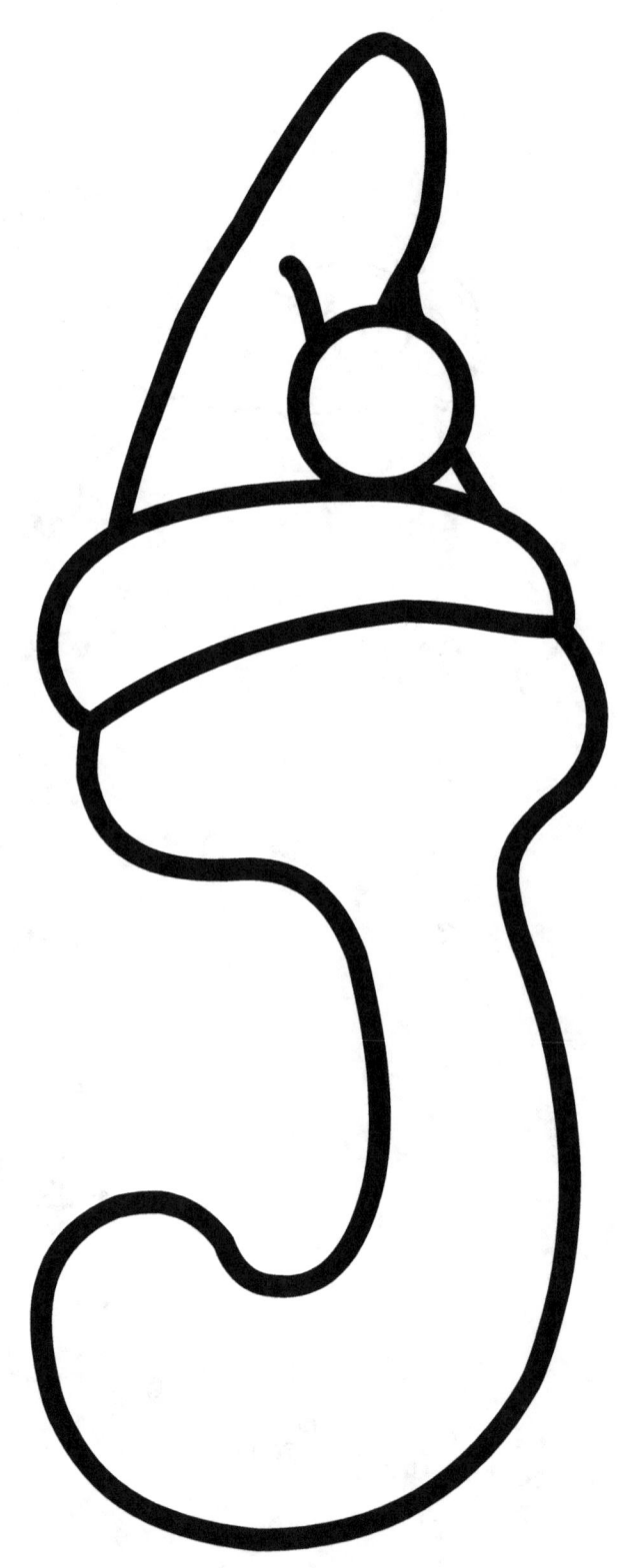

 J j

CONNECT THE DOTS

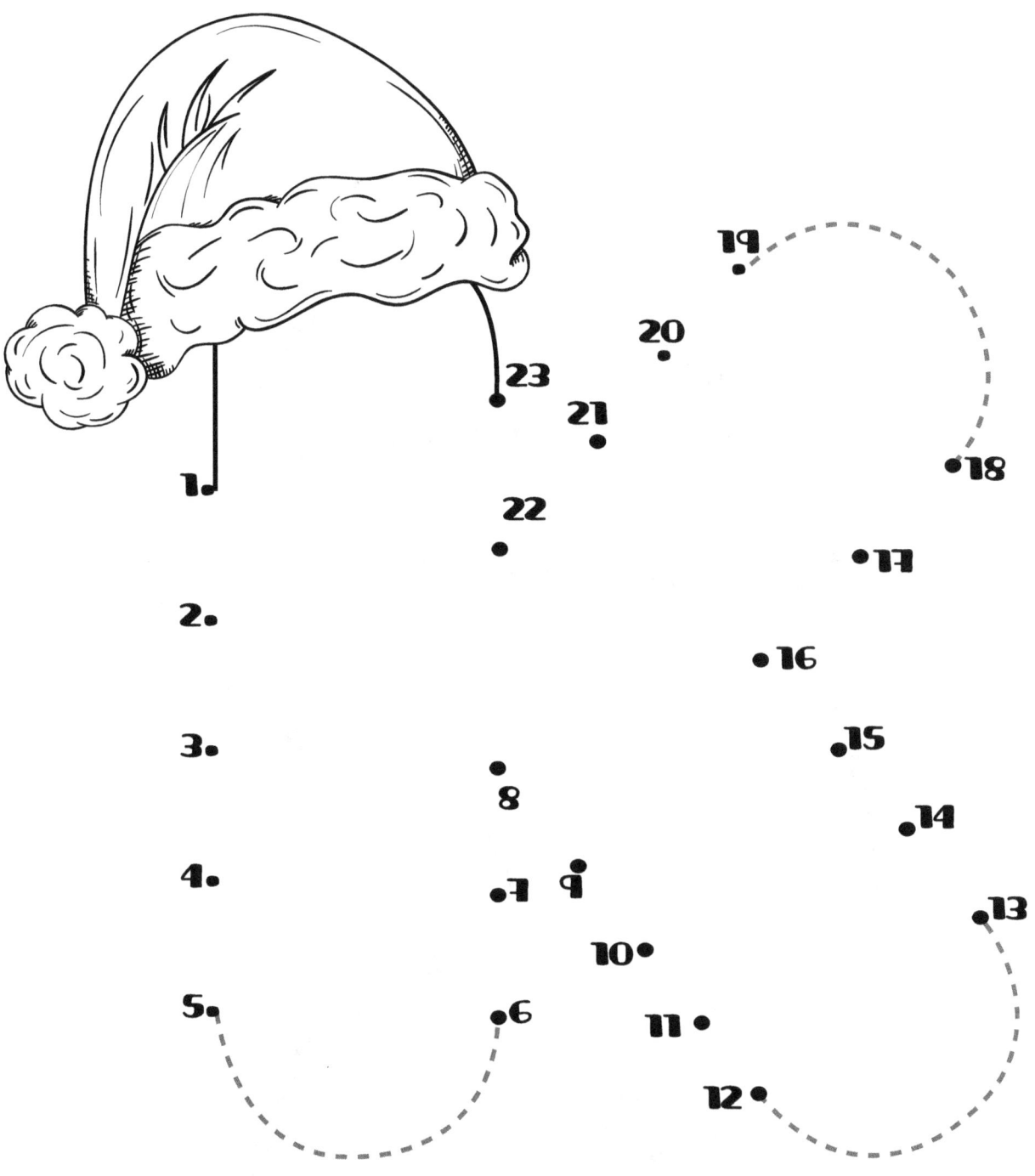

K COLOR IT

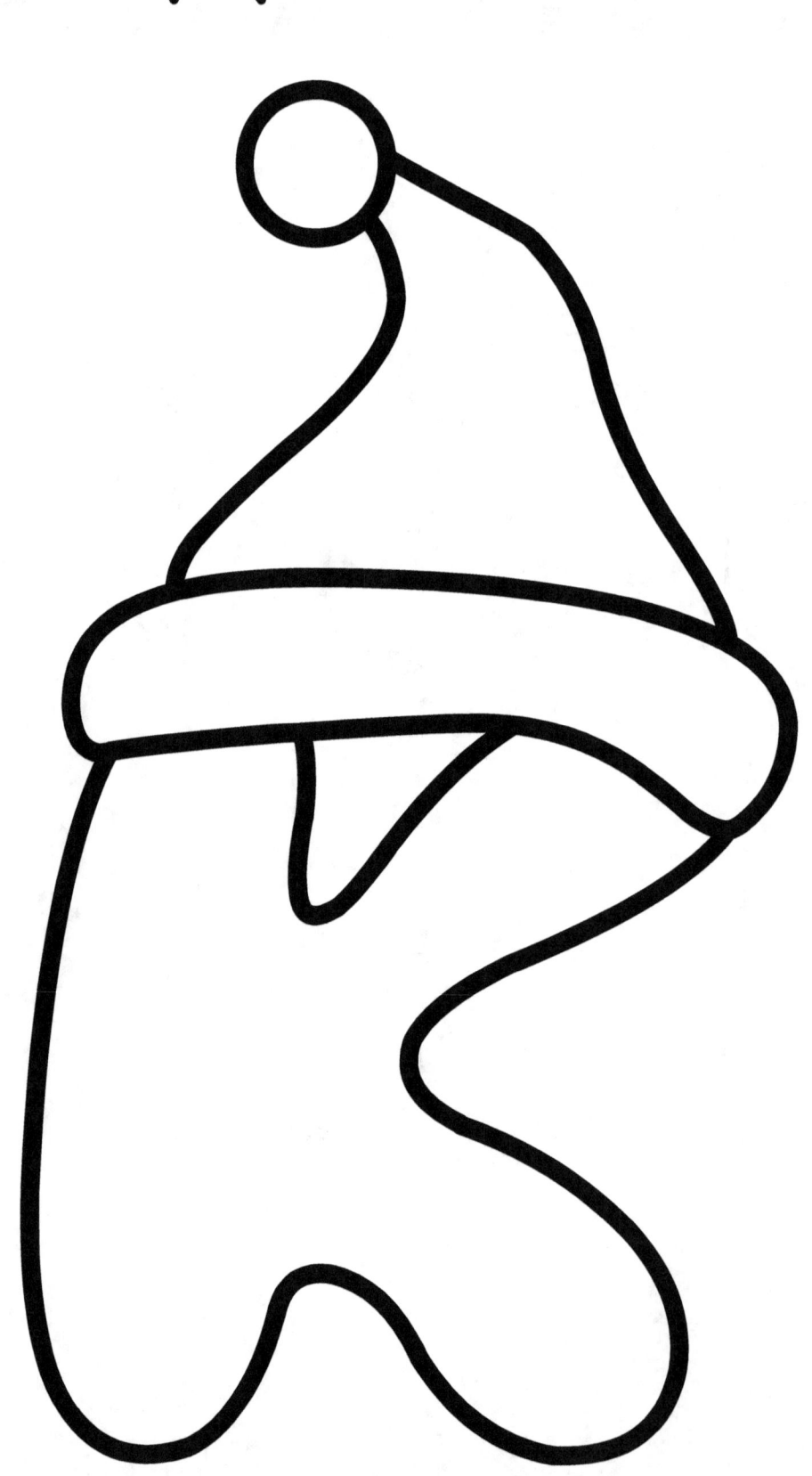

K k

CONNECT THE DOTS

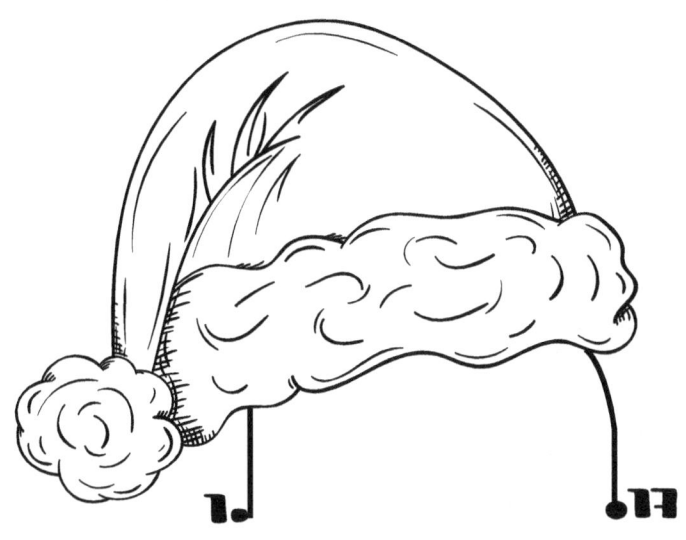

1. • •17

2. • •16

3. • •15

4. • •14

           •13   •12   •11
5. •

6. •

        •7   •8   •9   •10

L COLOR IT

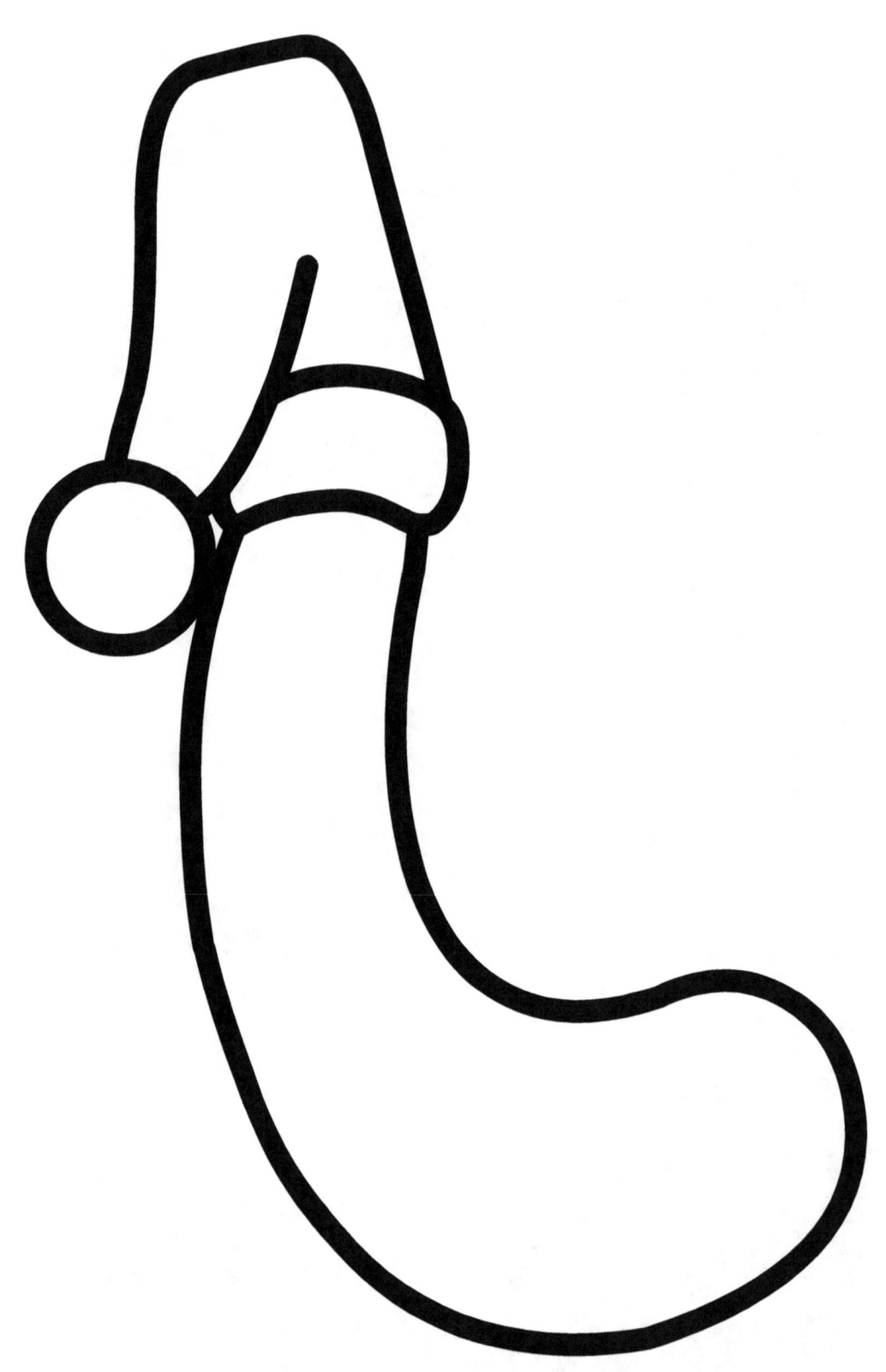

CONNECT THE DOTS

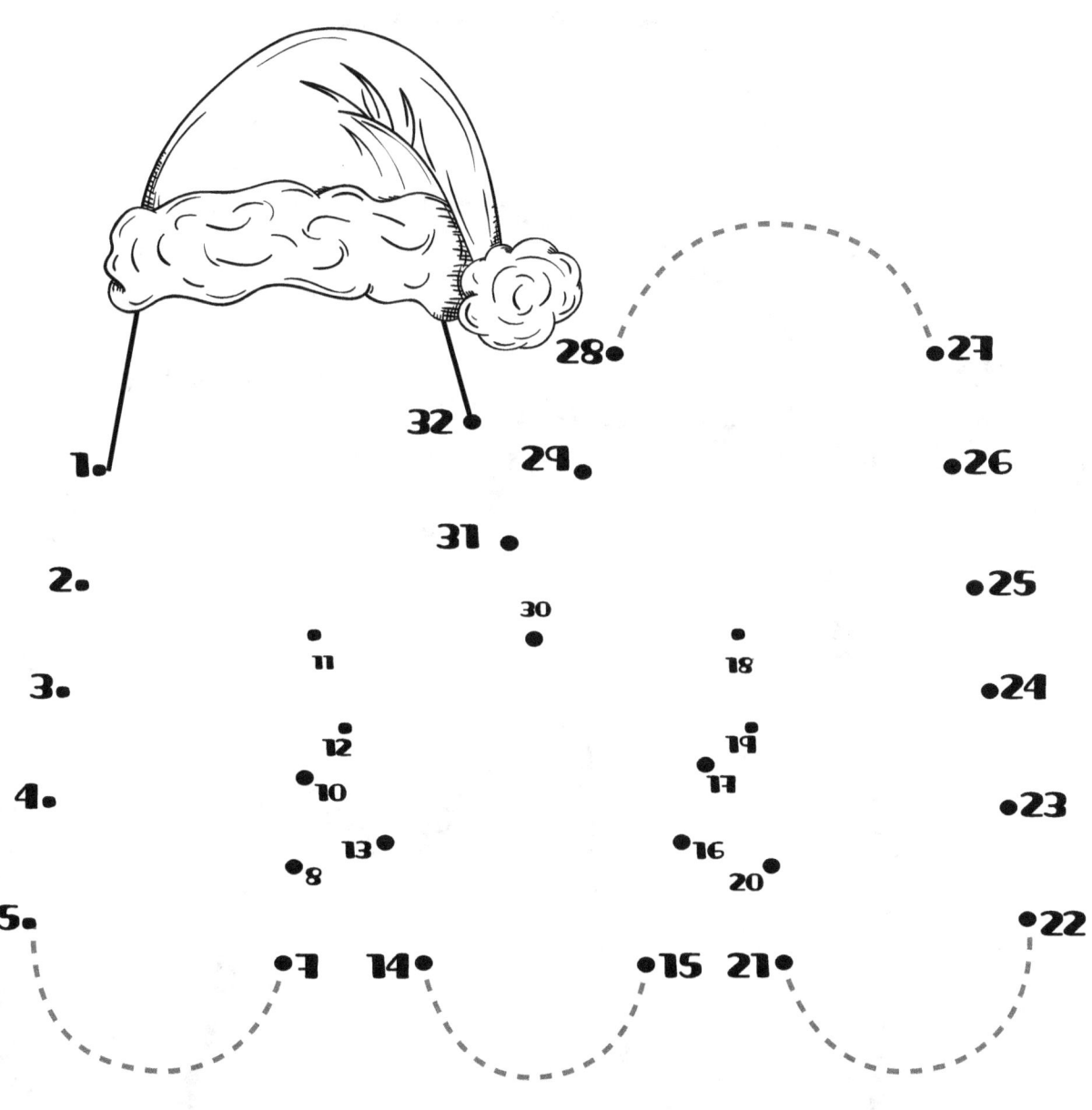

M COLOR IT

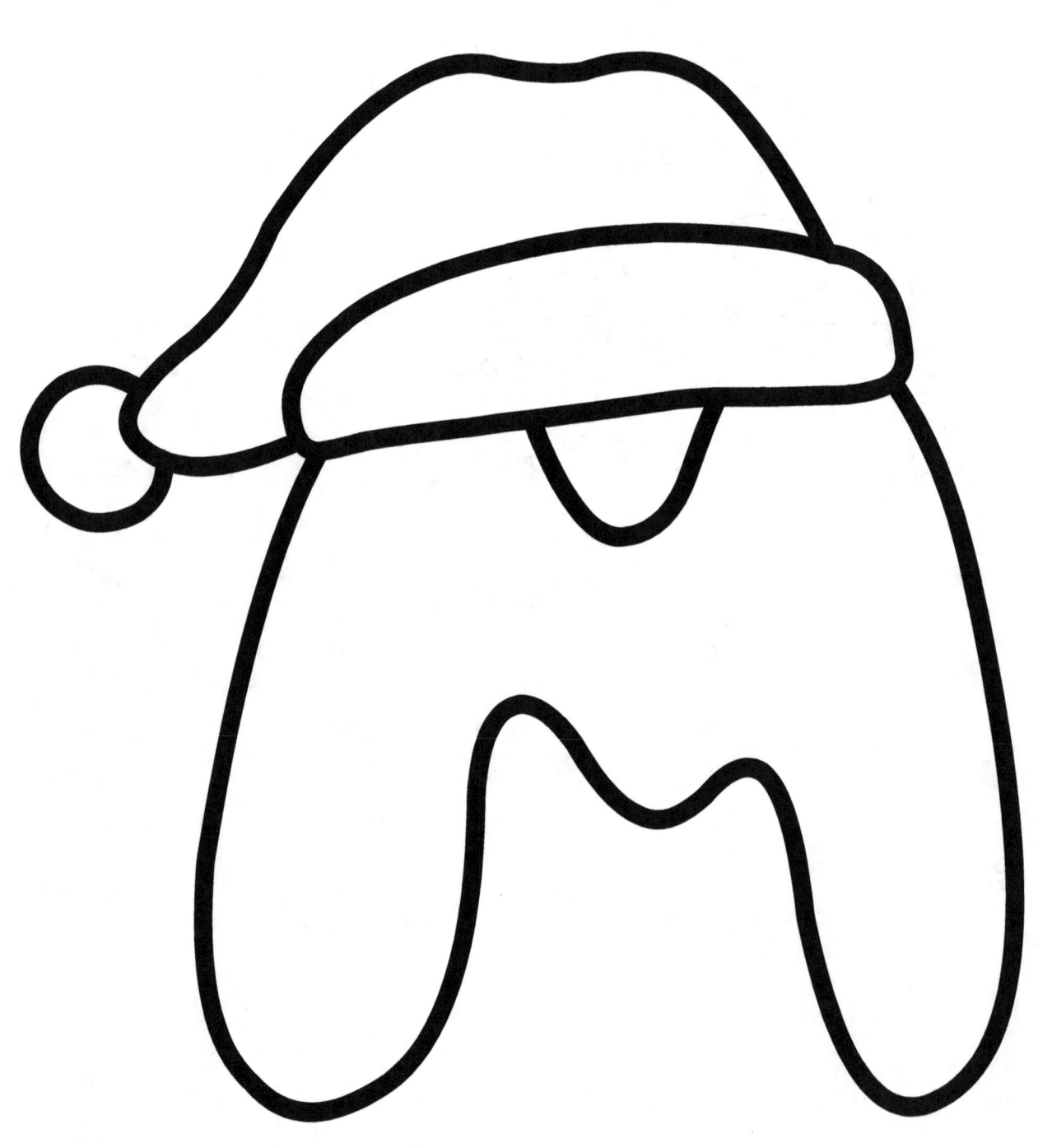

M m

CONNECT THE DOTS

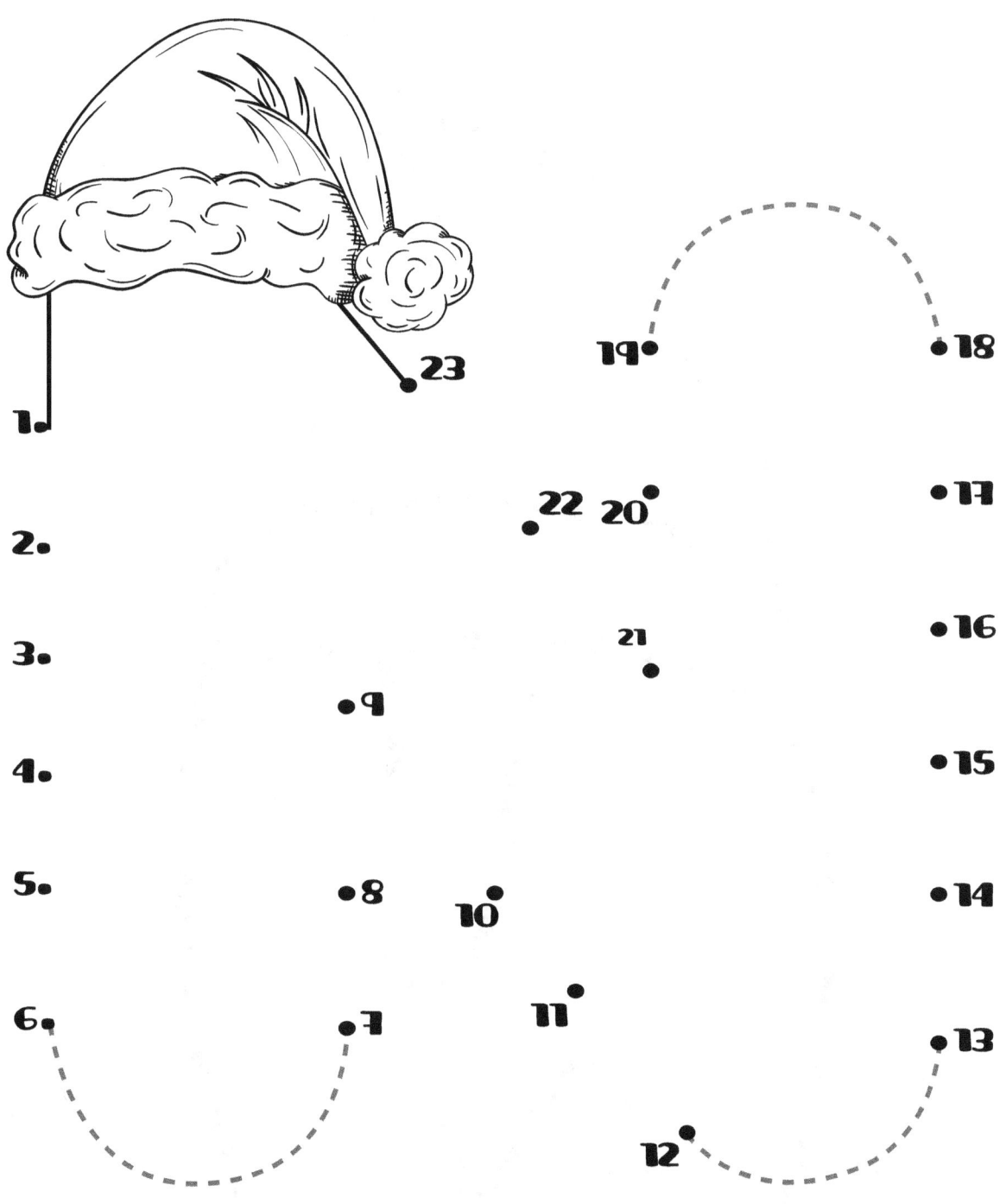

N COLOR IT

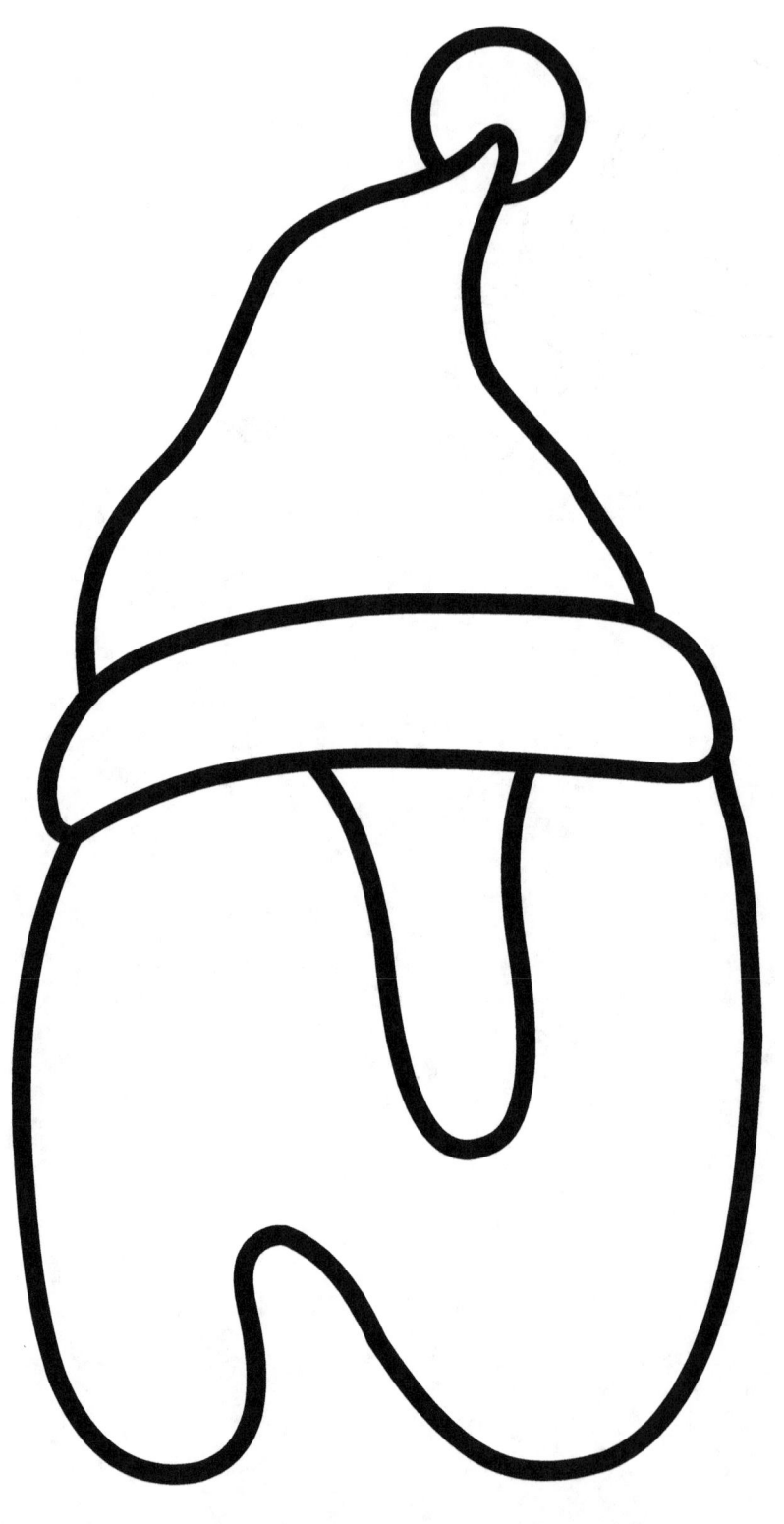

# N n

CONNECT THE DOTS

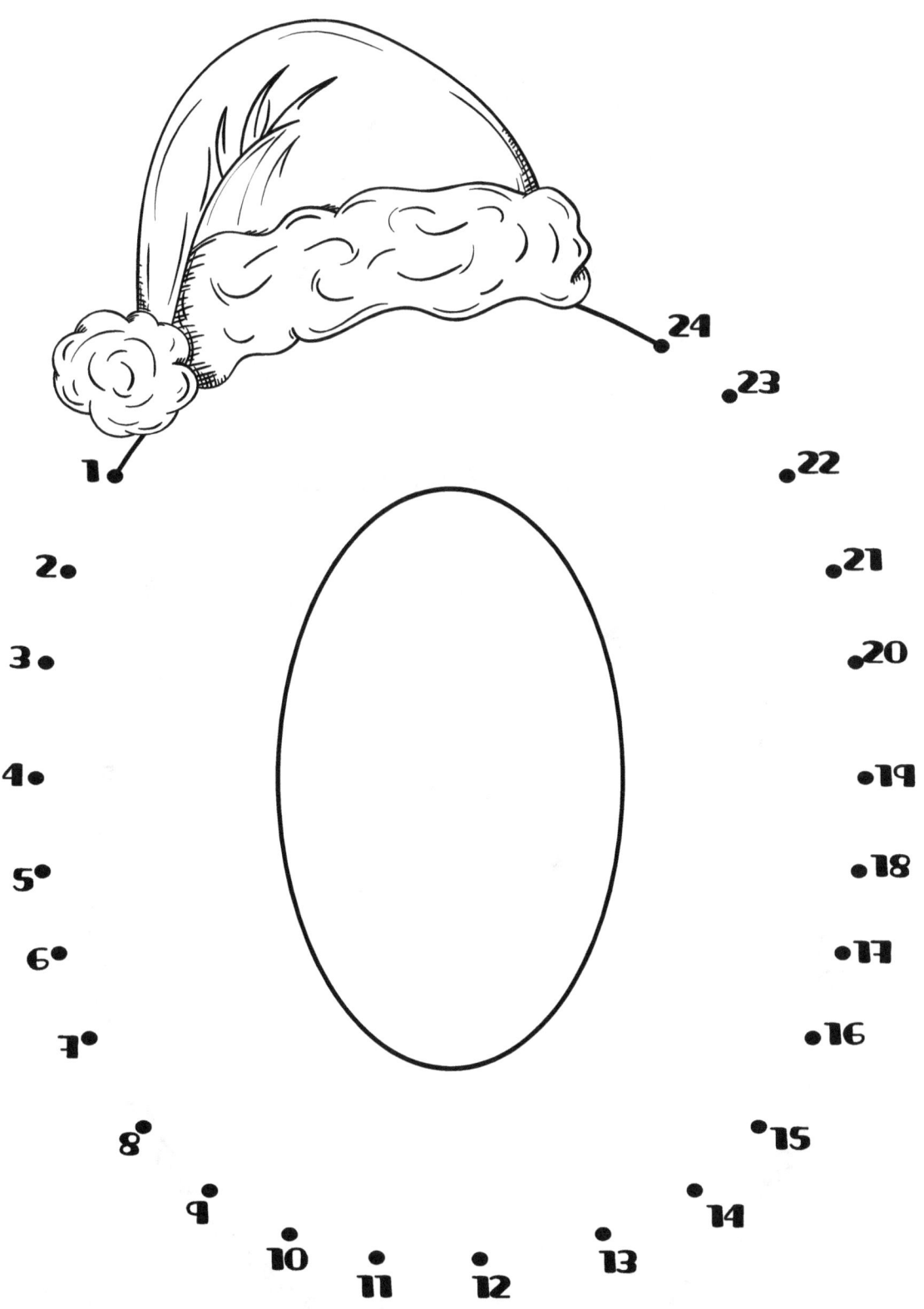

○ COLOR IT

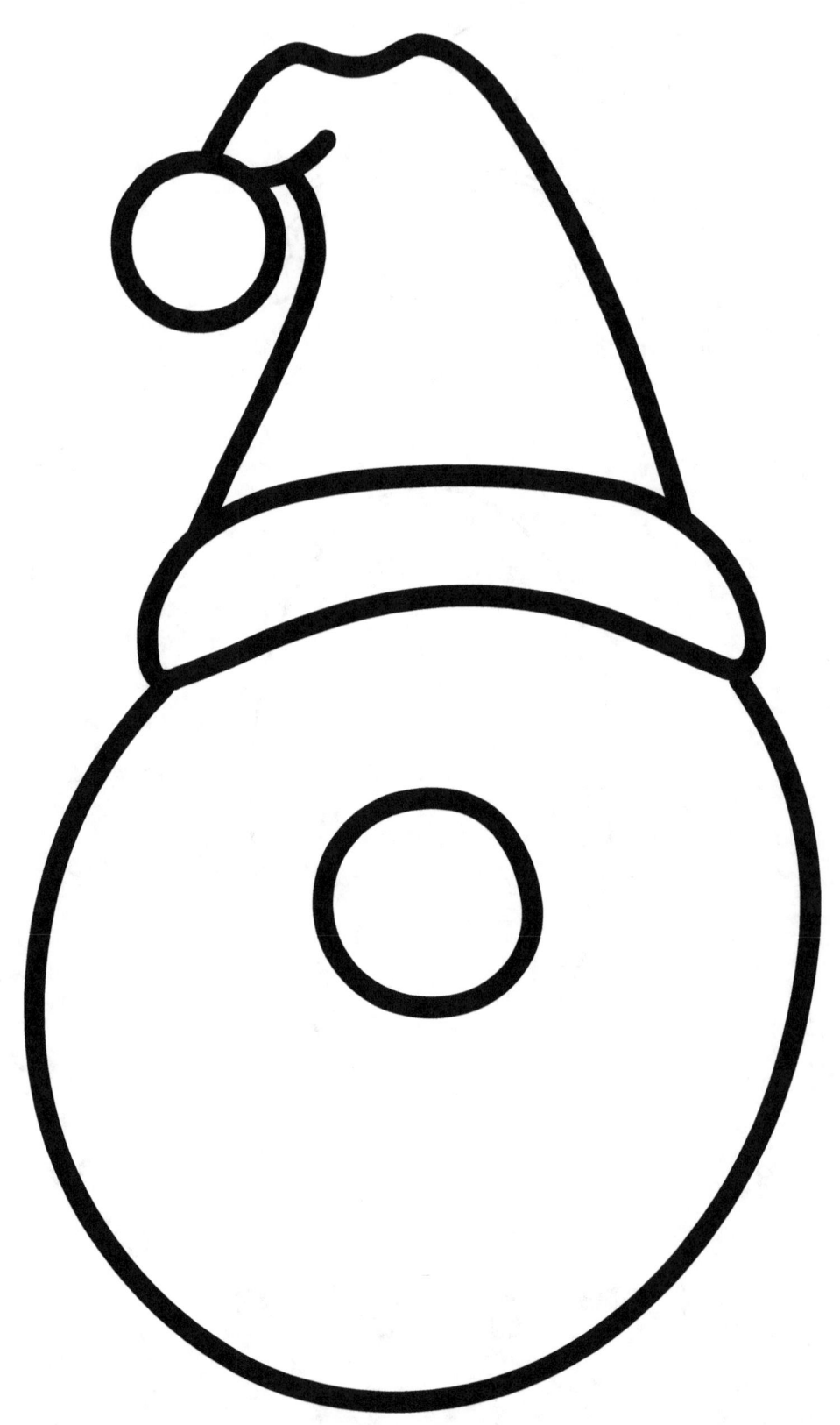

CONNECT THE DOTS

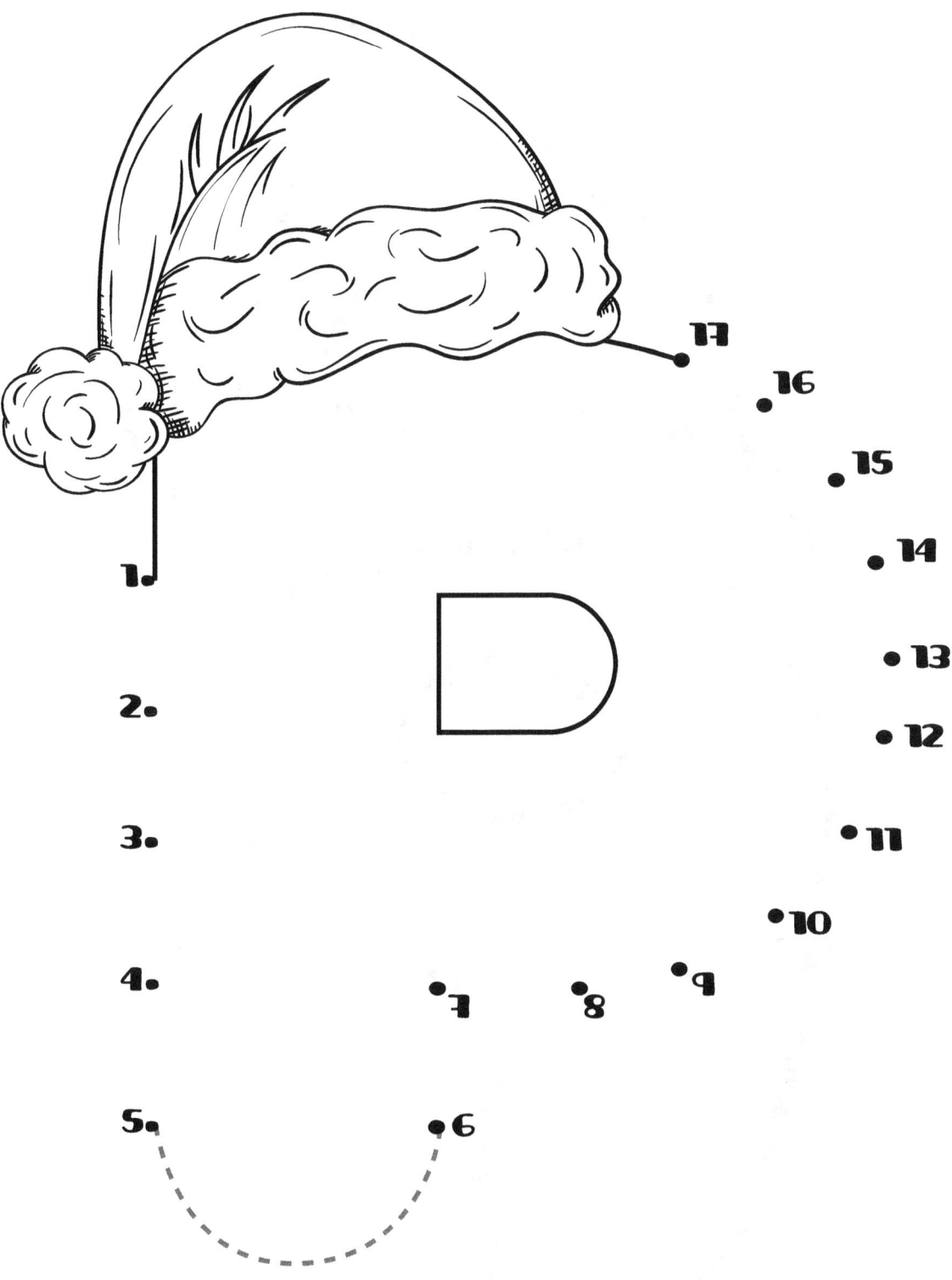

P COLOR IT

CONNECT THE DOTS

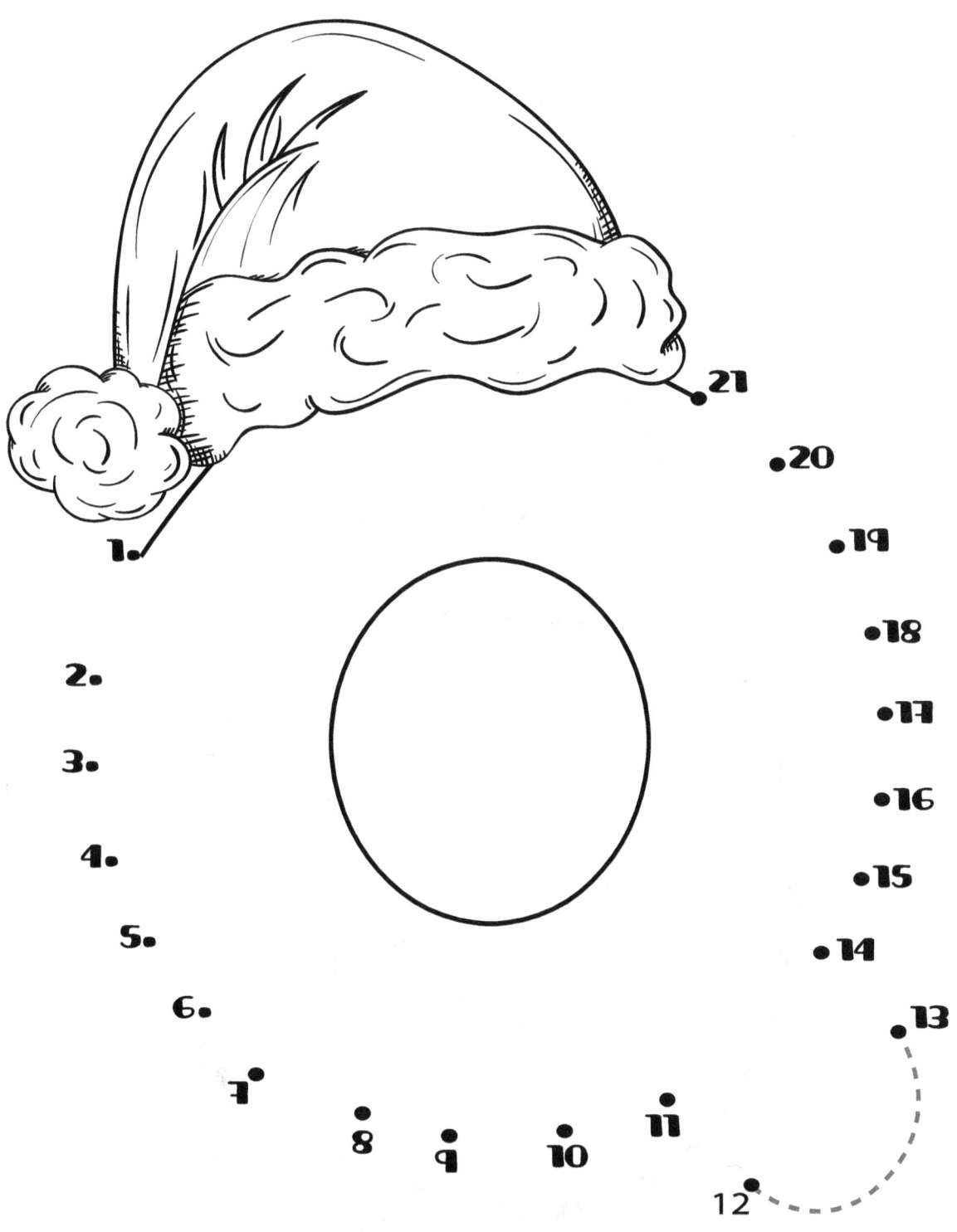

Q COLOR IT

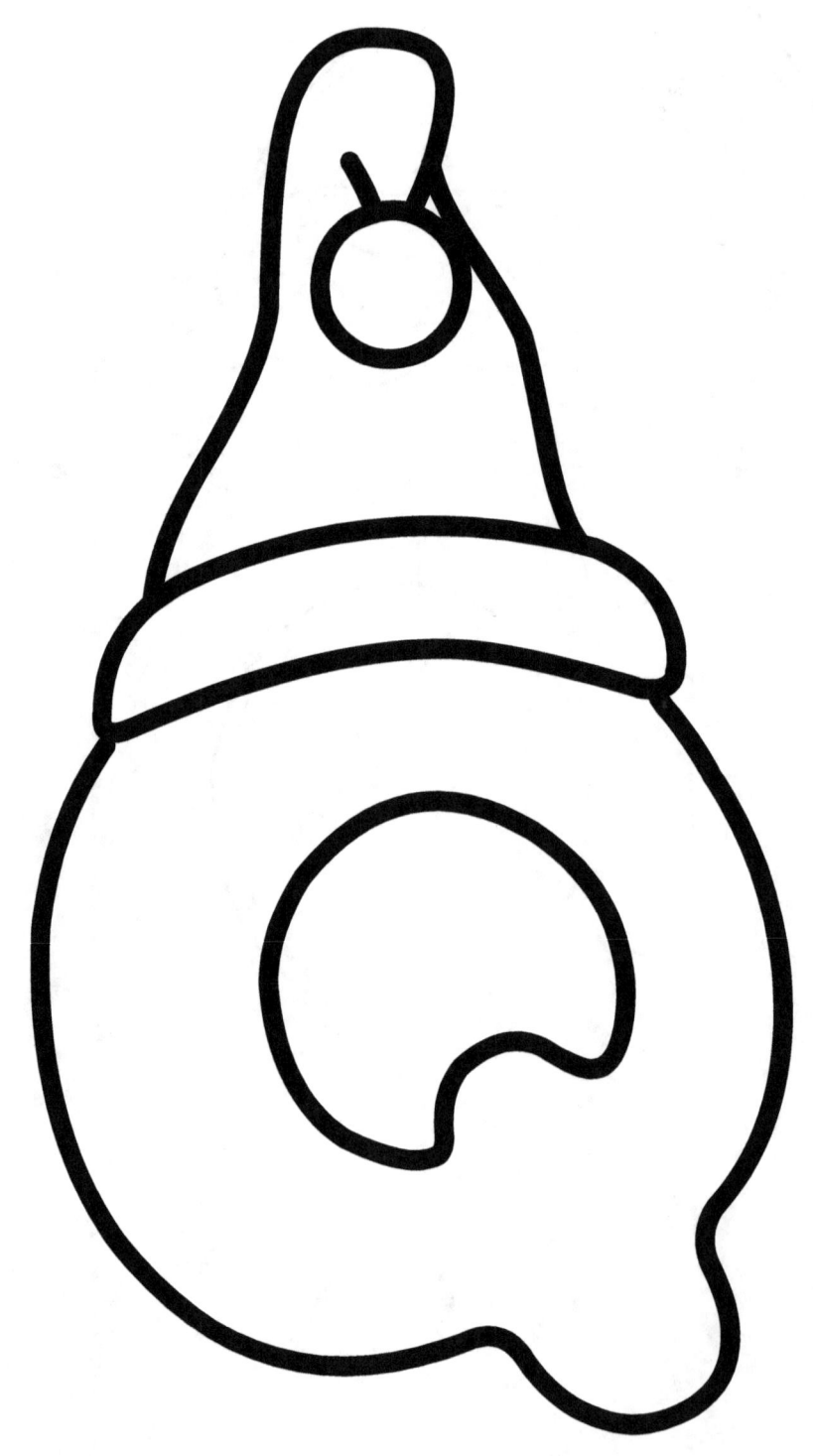

CONNECT THE DOTS

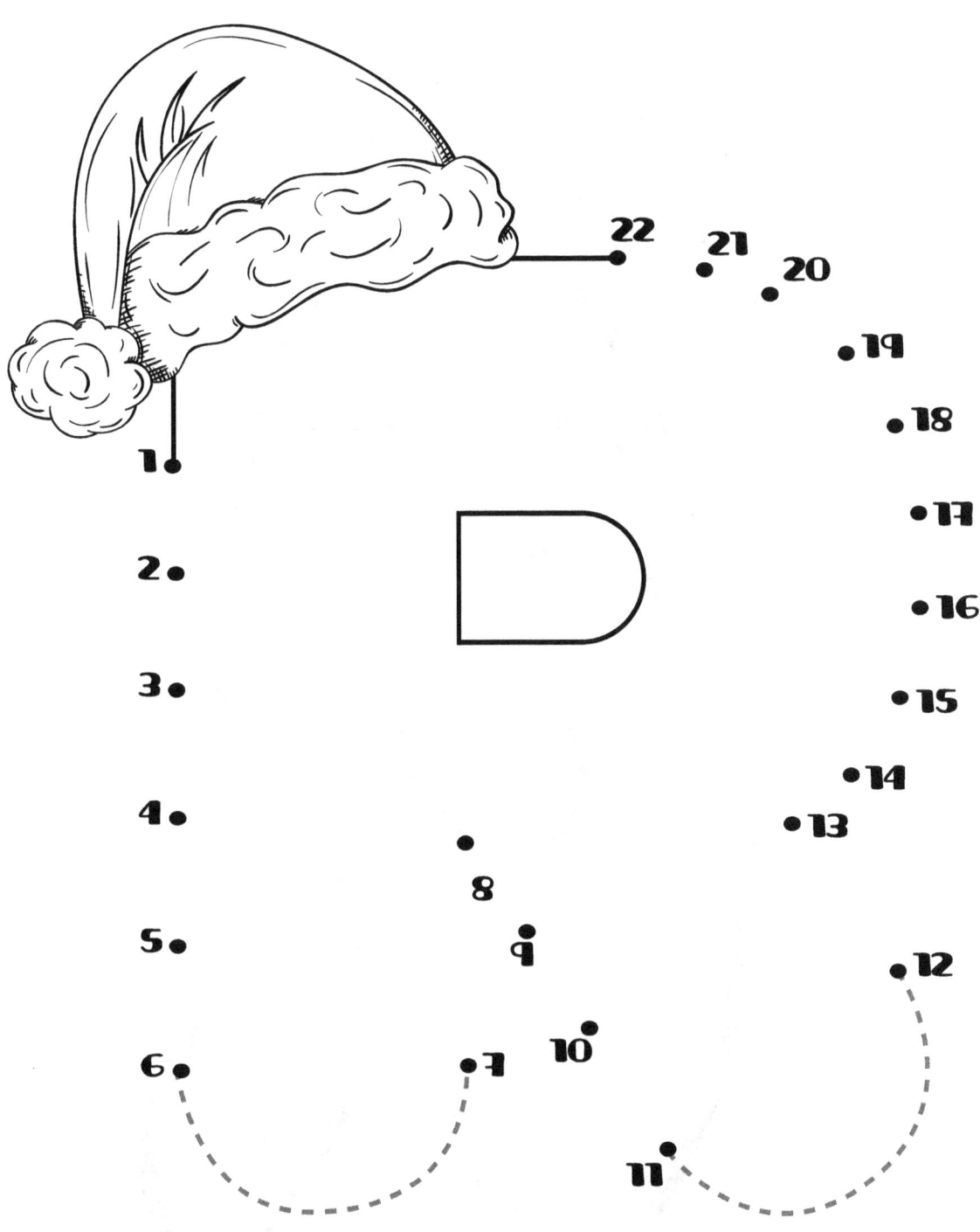

R COLOR IT

CONNECT THE DOTS

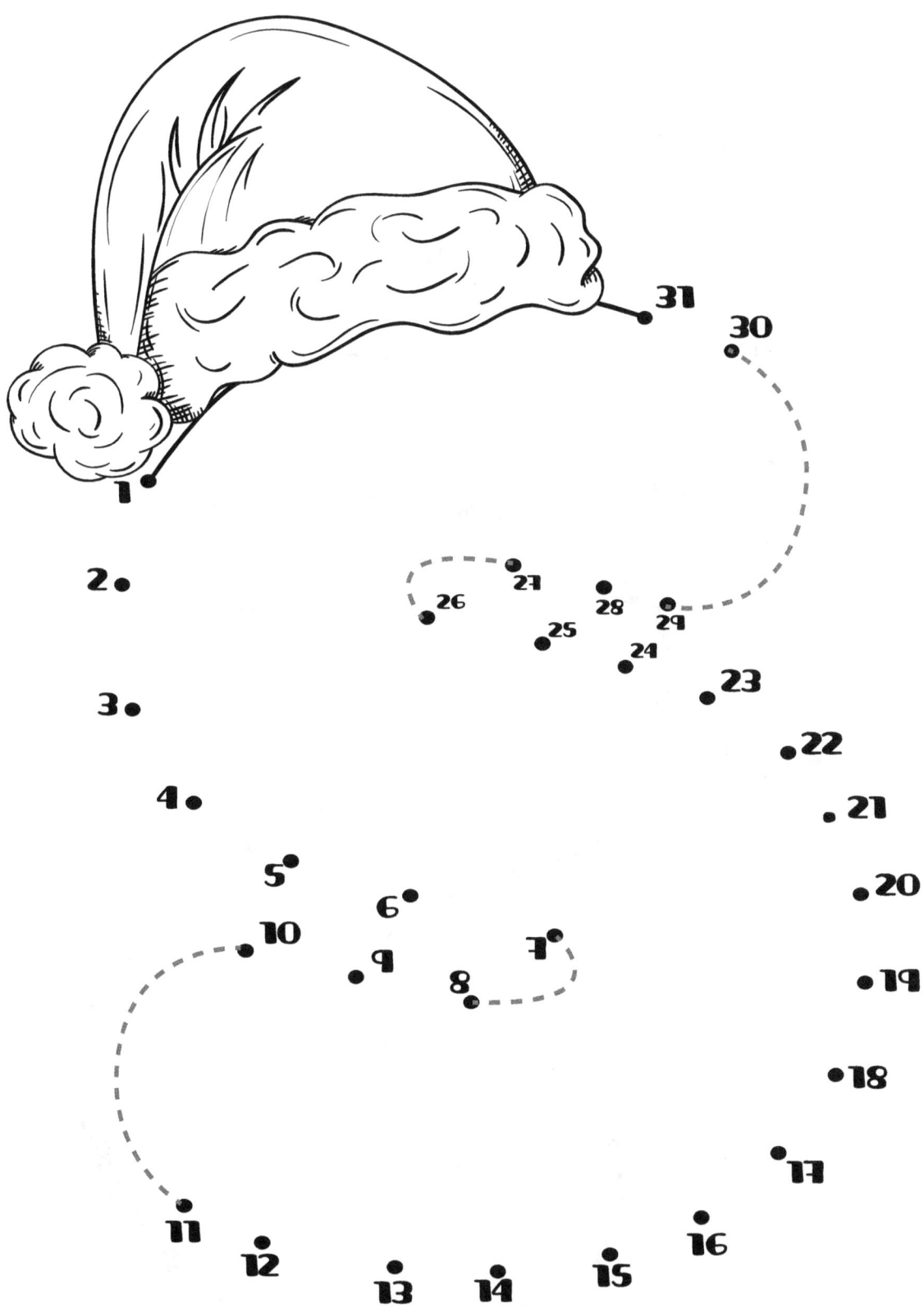

S COLOR IT

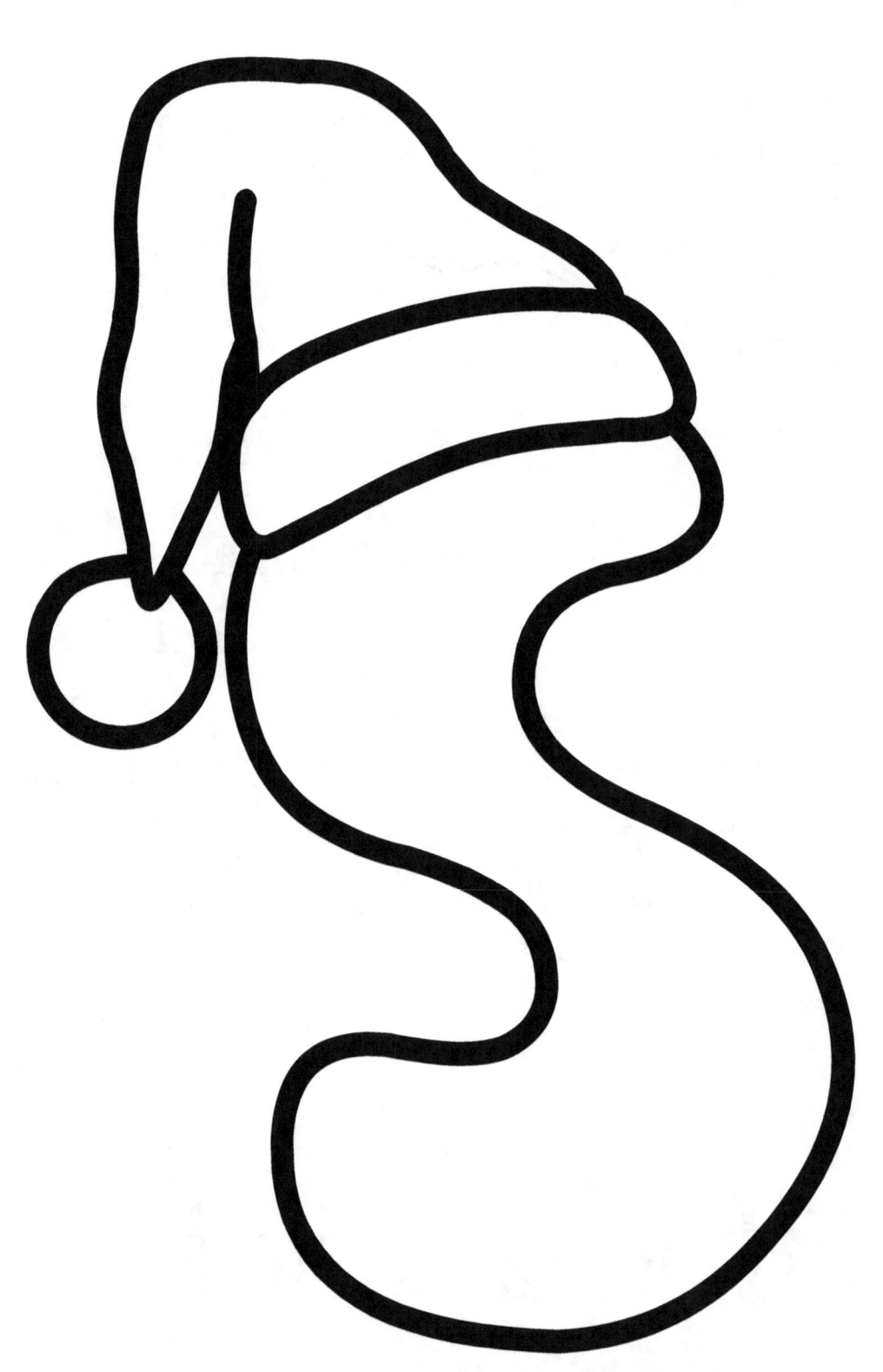

 # S s

CONNECT THE DOTS

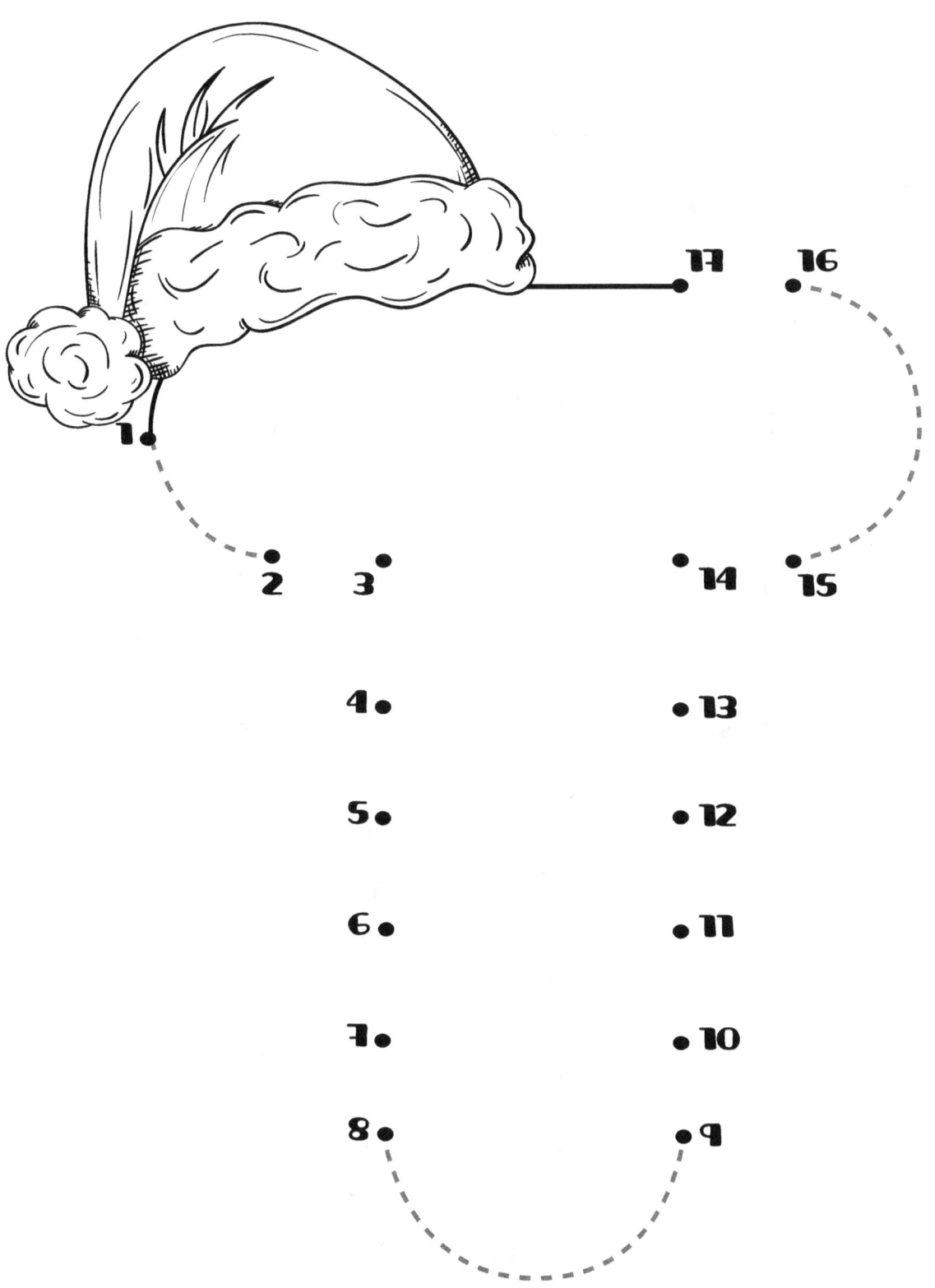

T COLOR IT

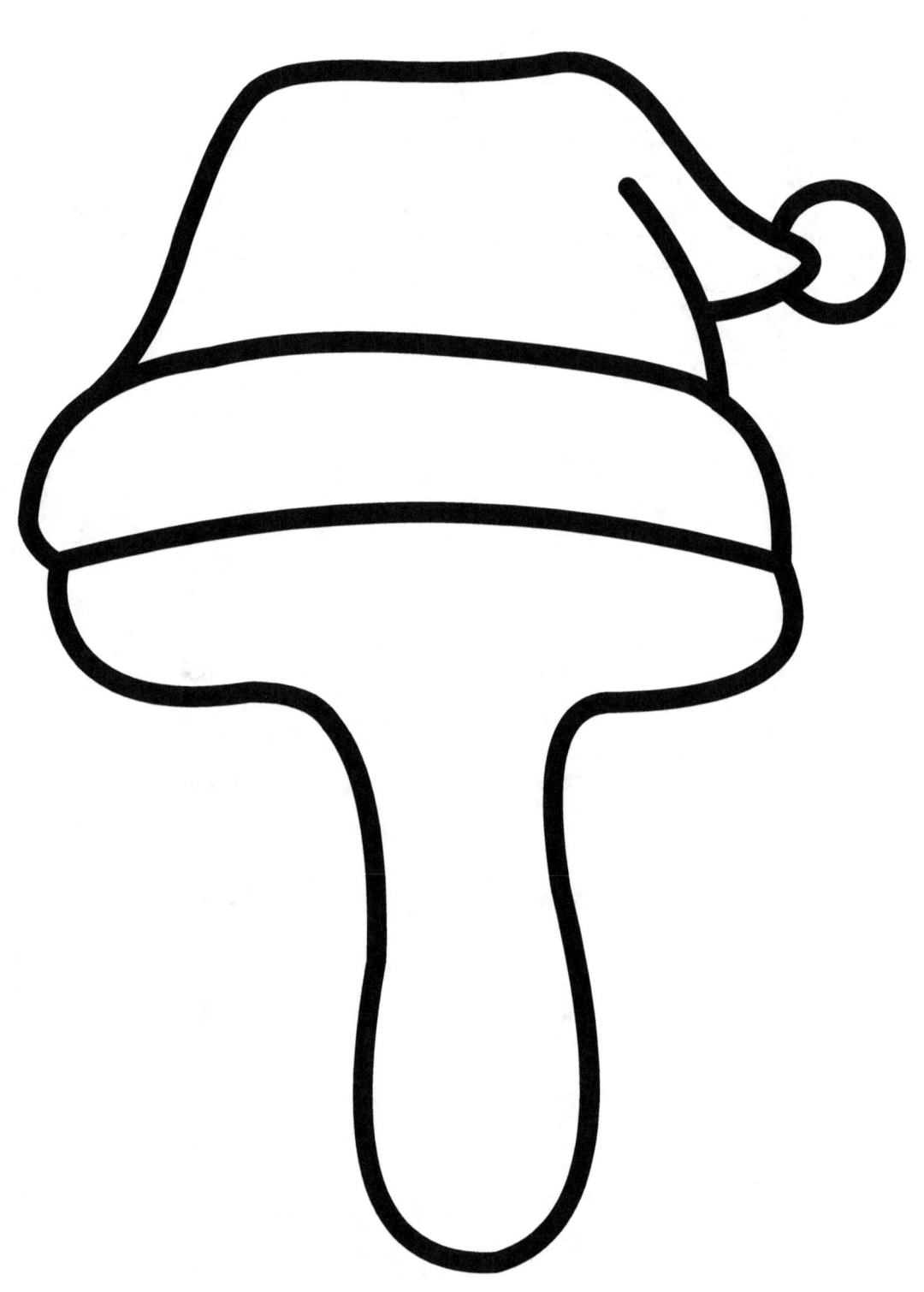

T t

CONNECT THE DOTS

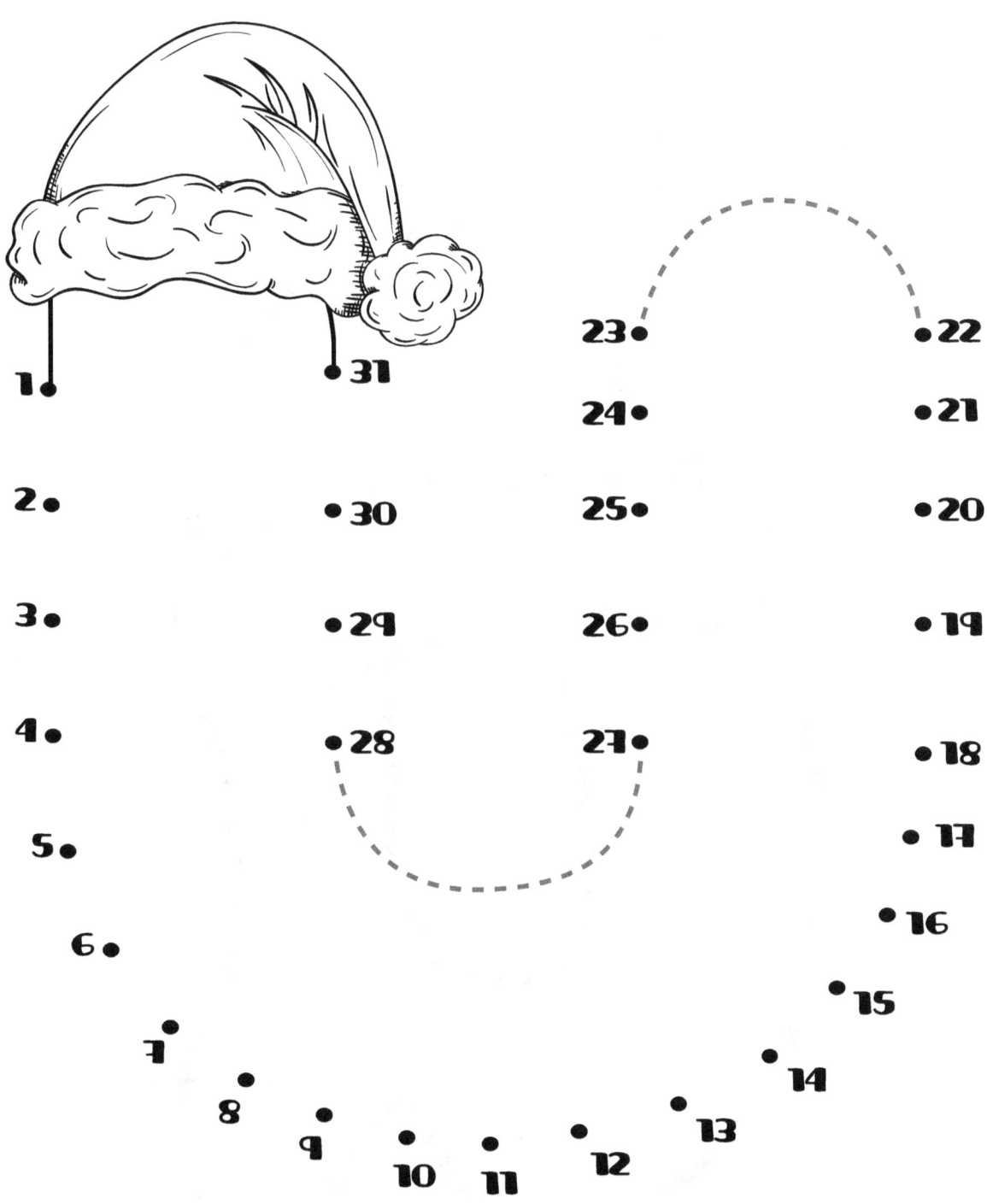

U COLOR IT

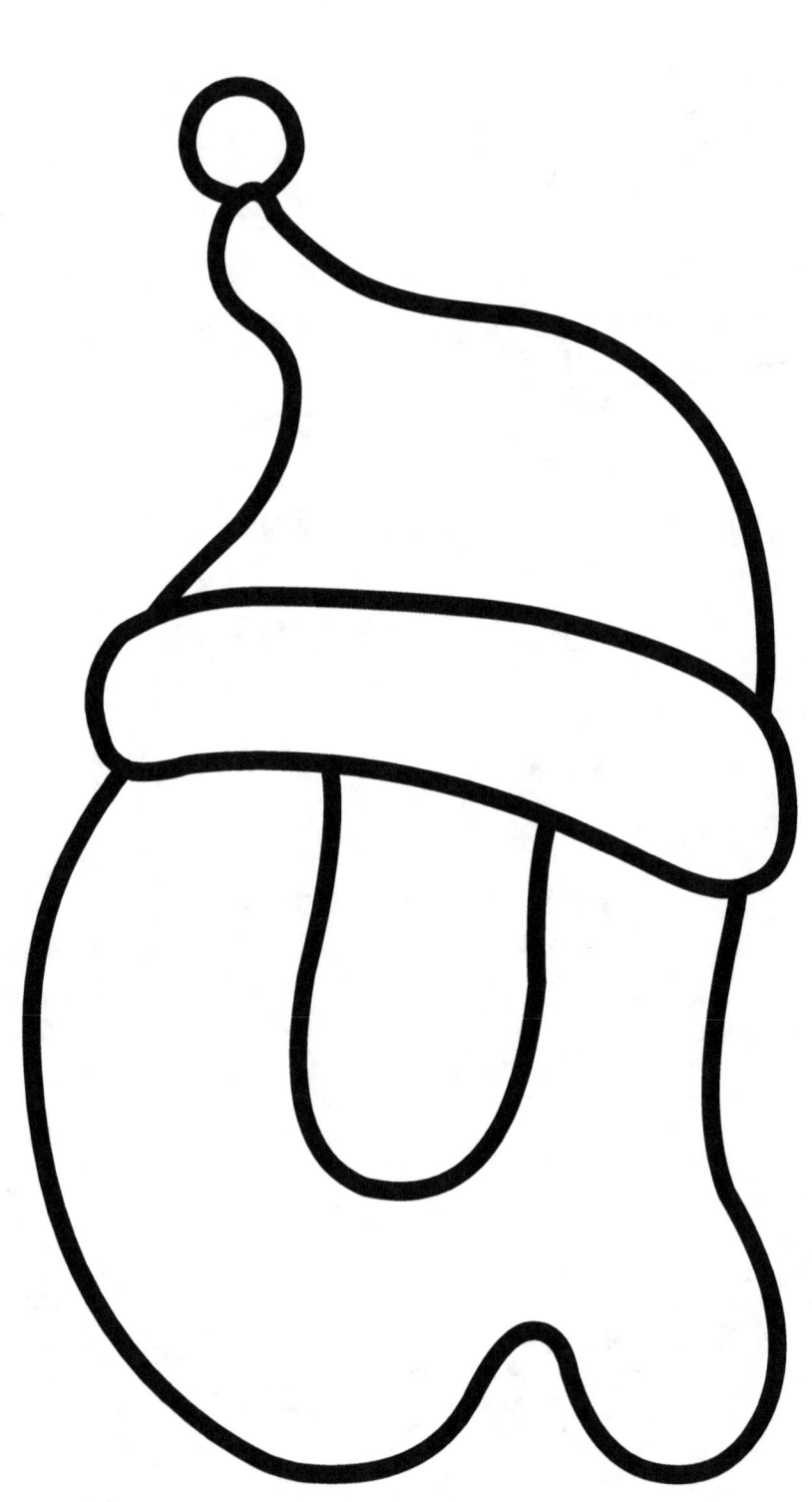

CONNECT THE DOTS

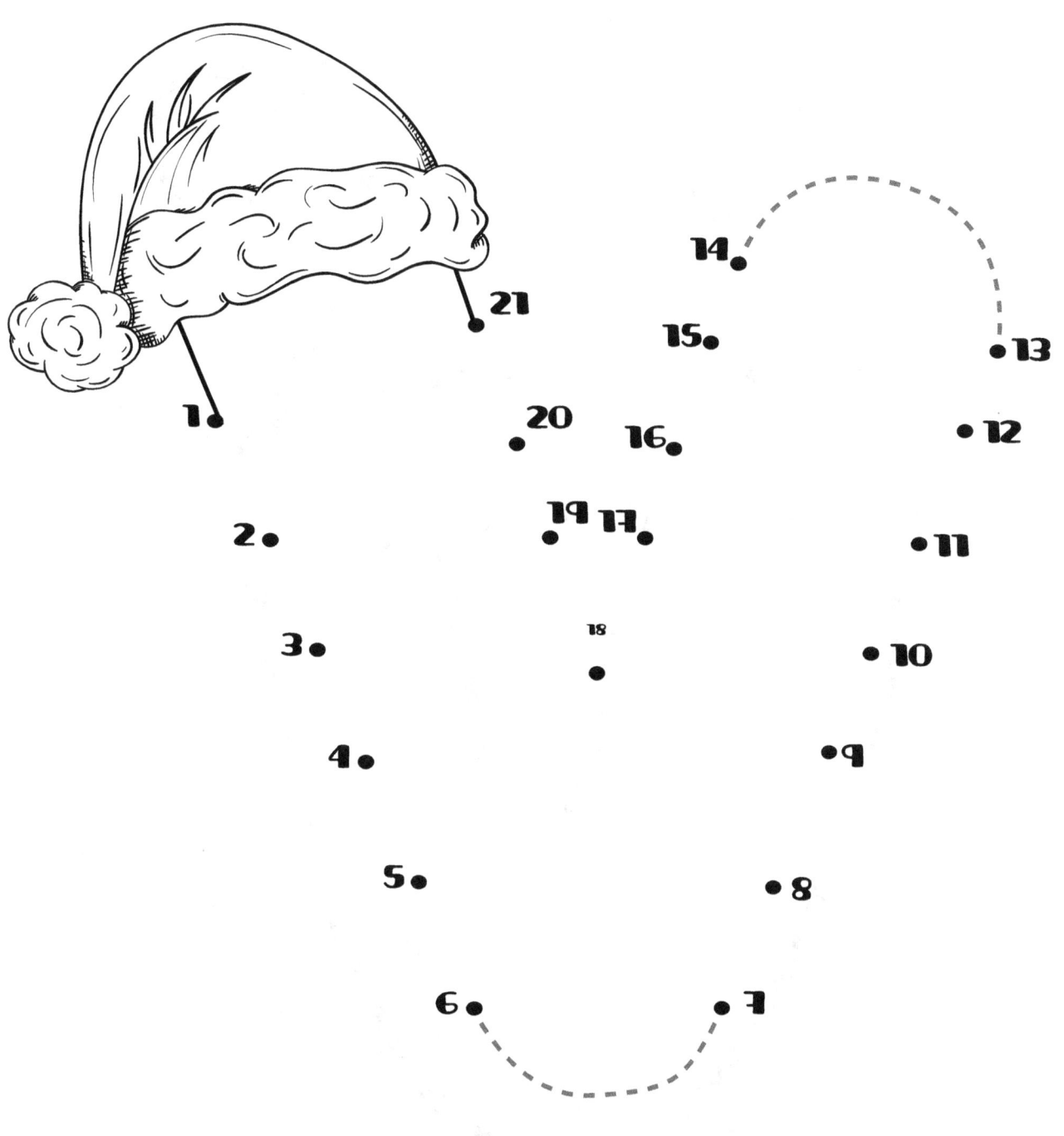

V COLOR IT

CONNECT THE DOTS

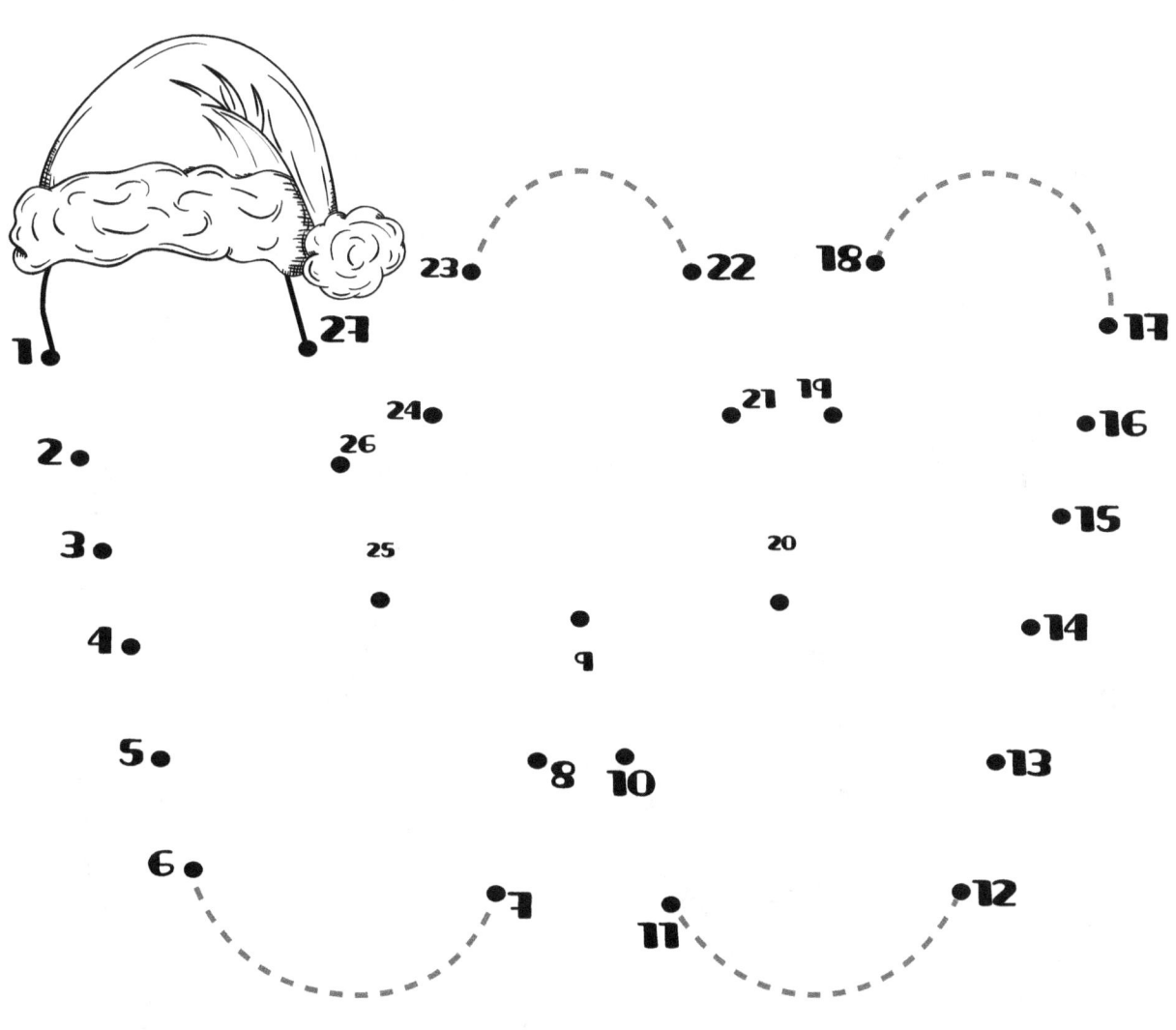

W COLOR IT

CONNECT THE DOTS

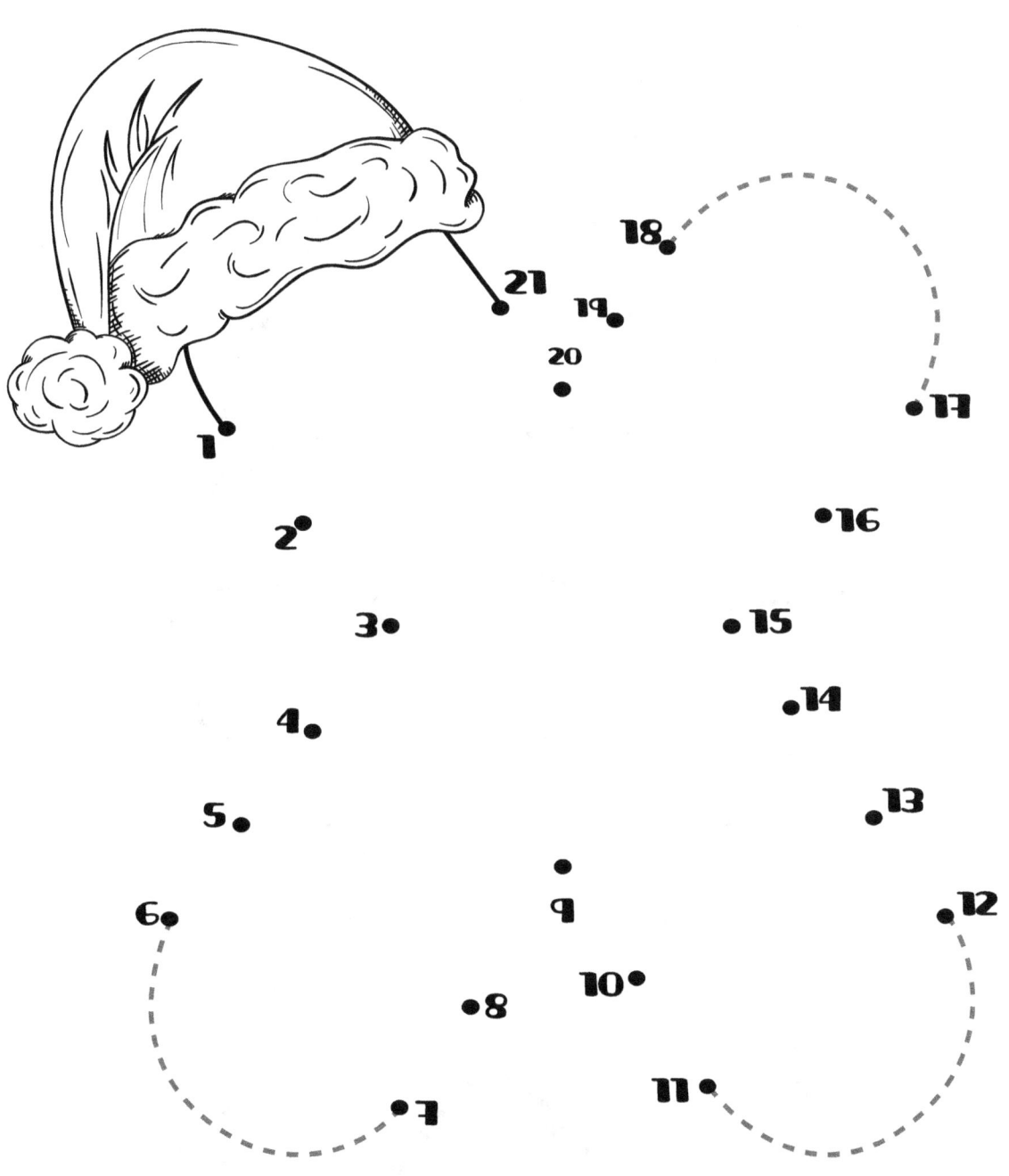

✗ COLOR IT

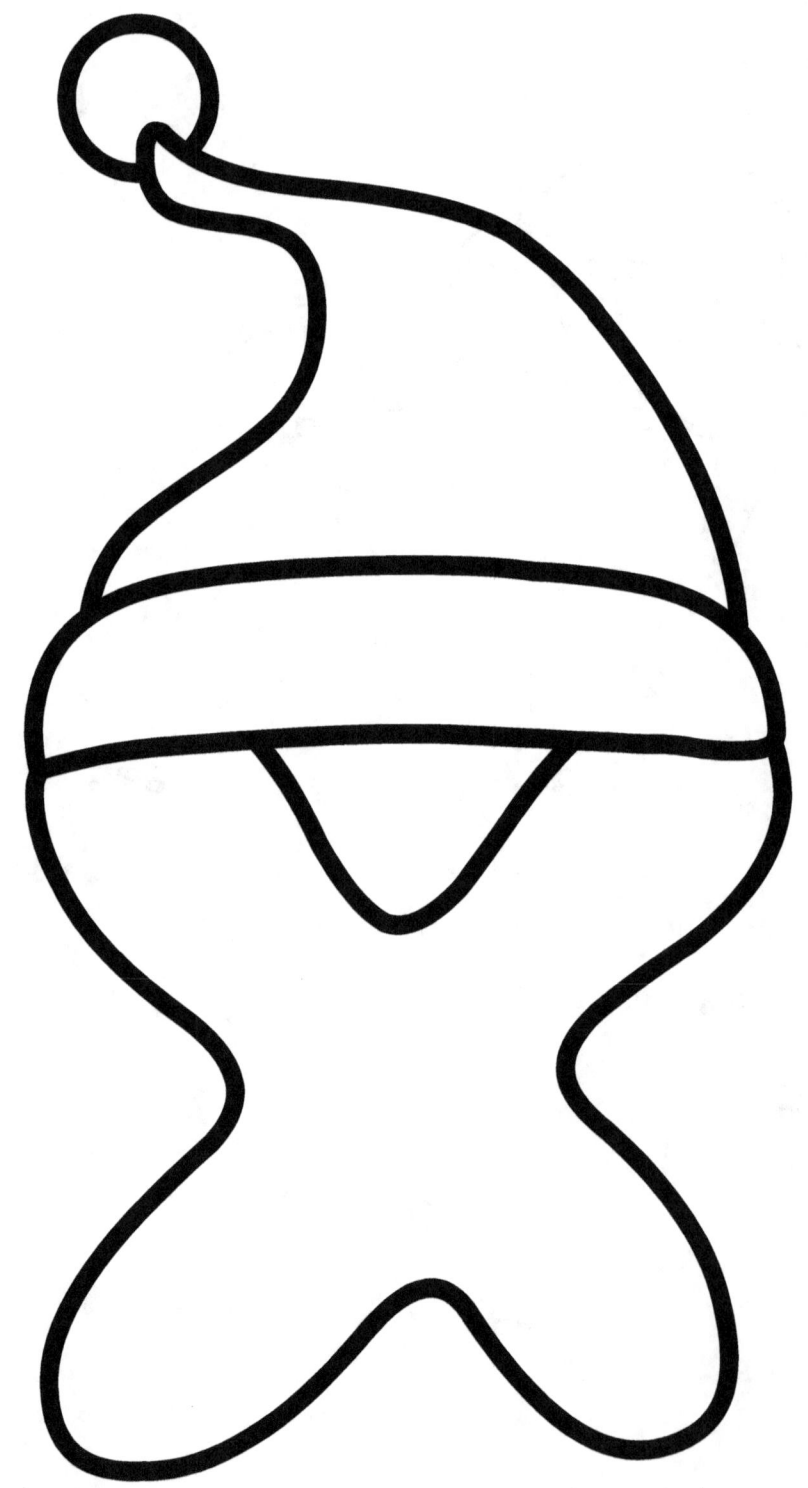

CONNECT THE DOTS

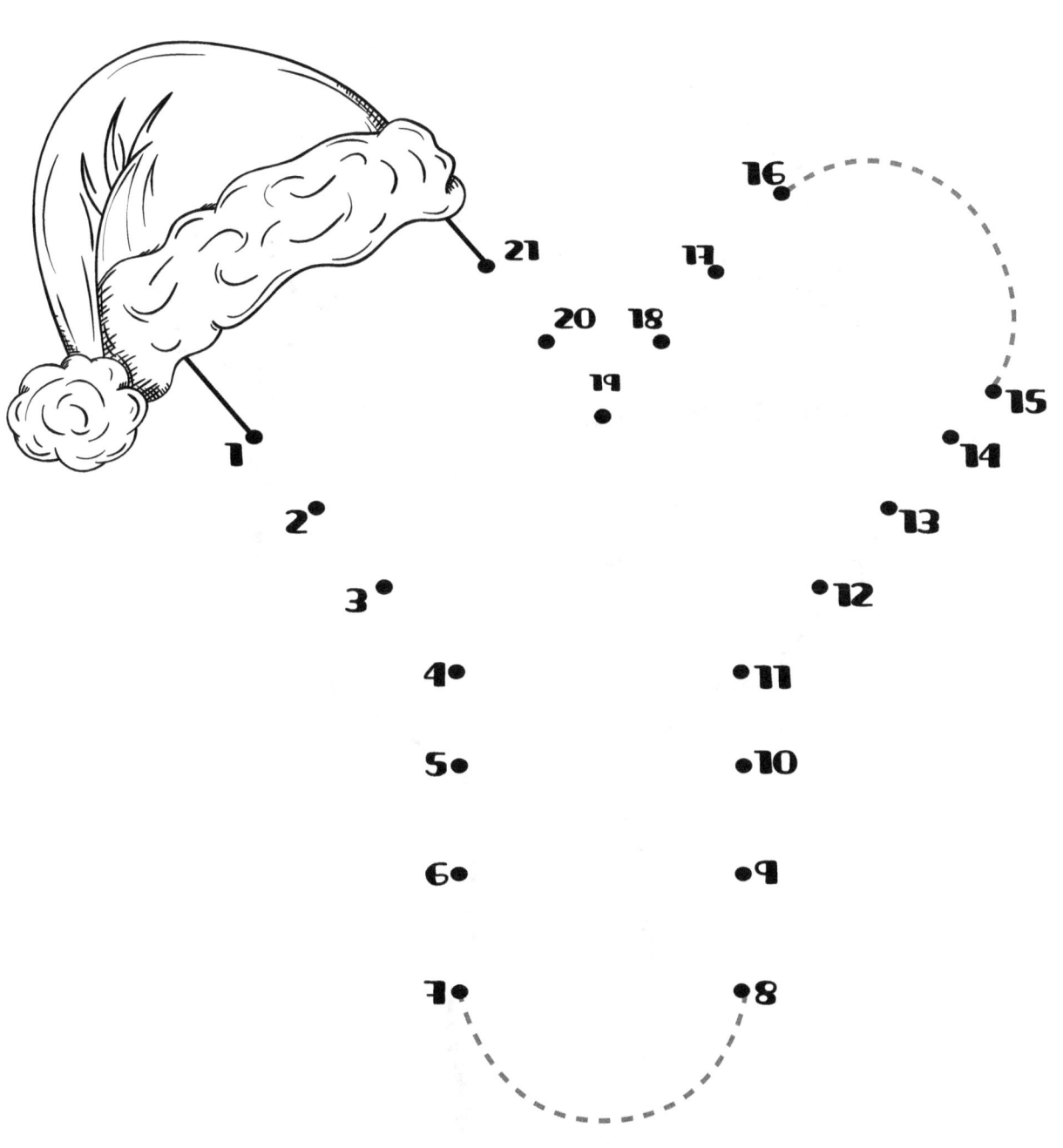

Y COLOR IT

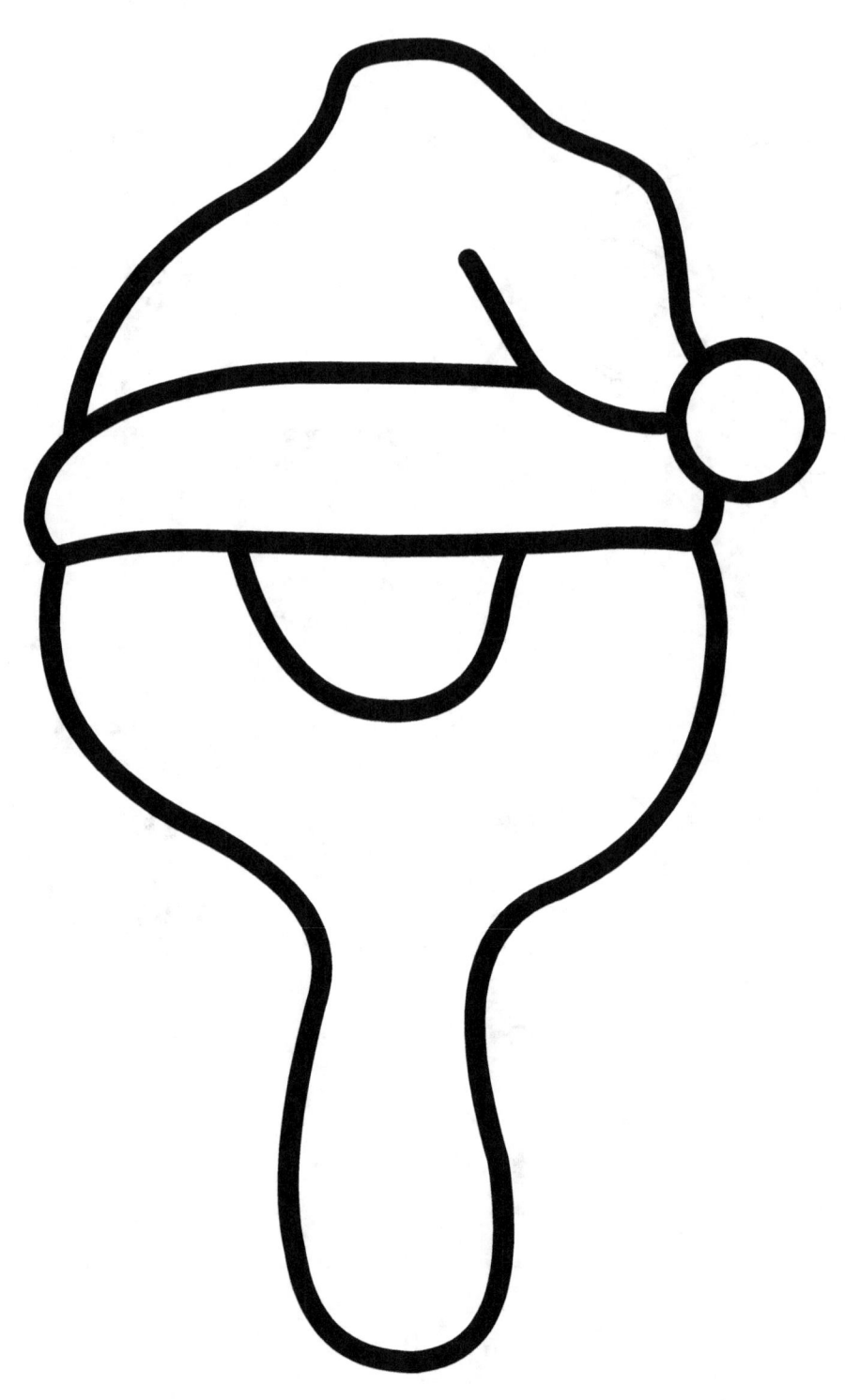

CONNECT THE DOTS

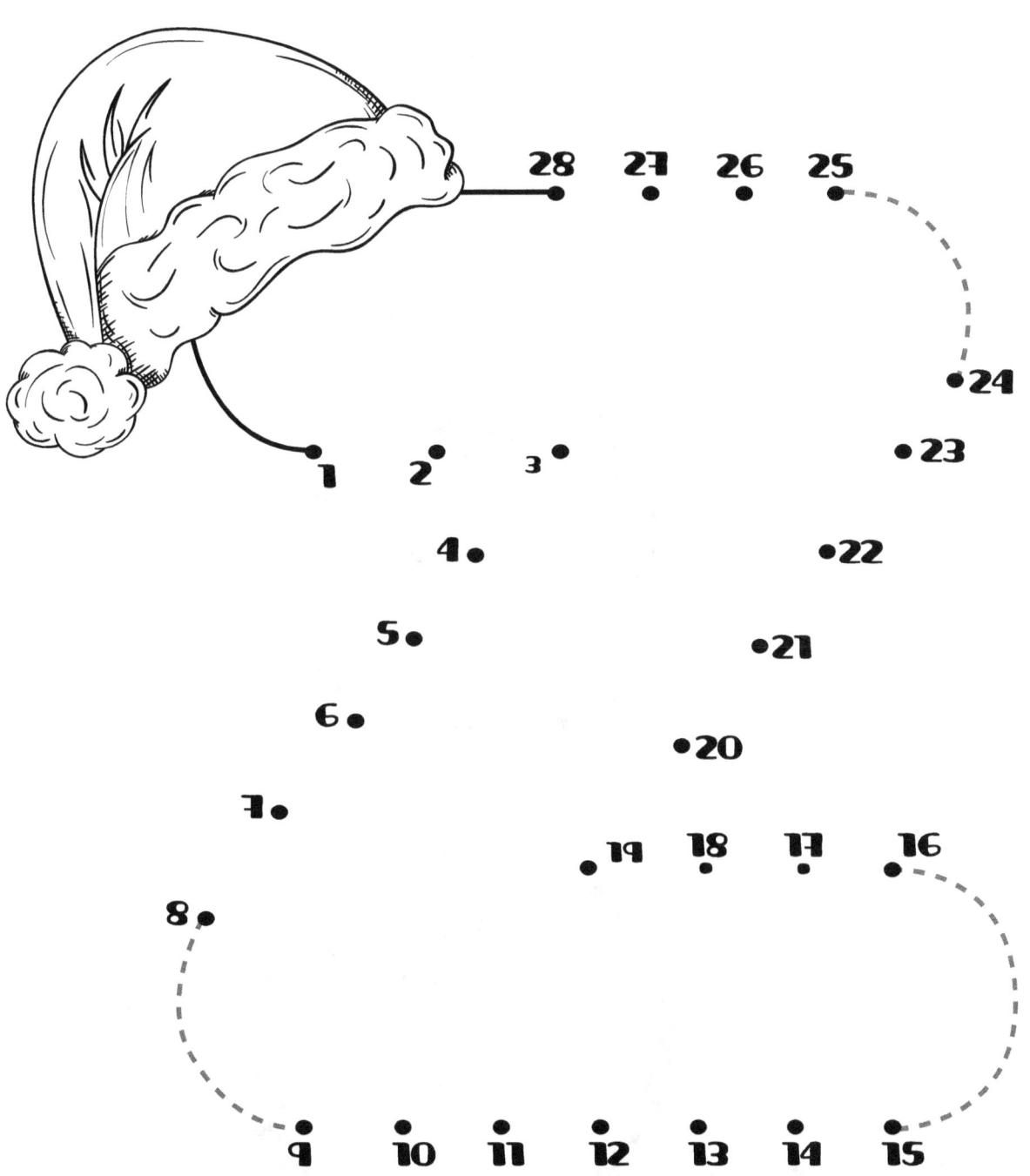

Z COLOR IT

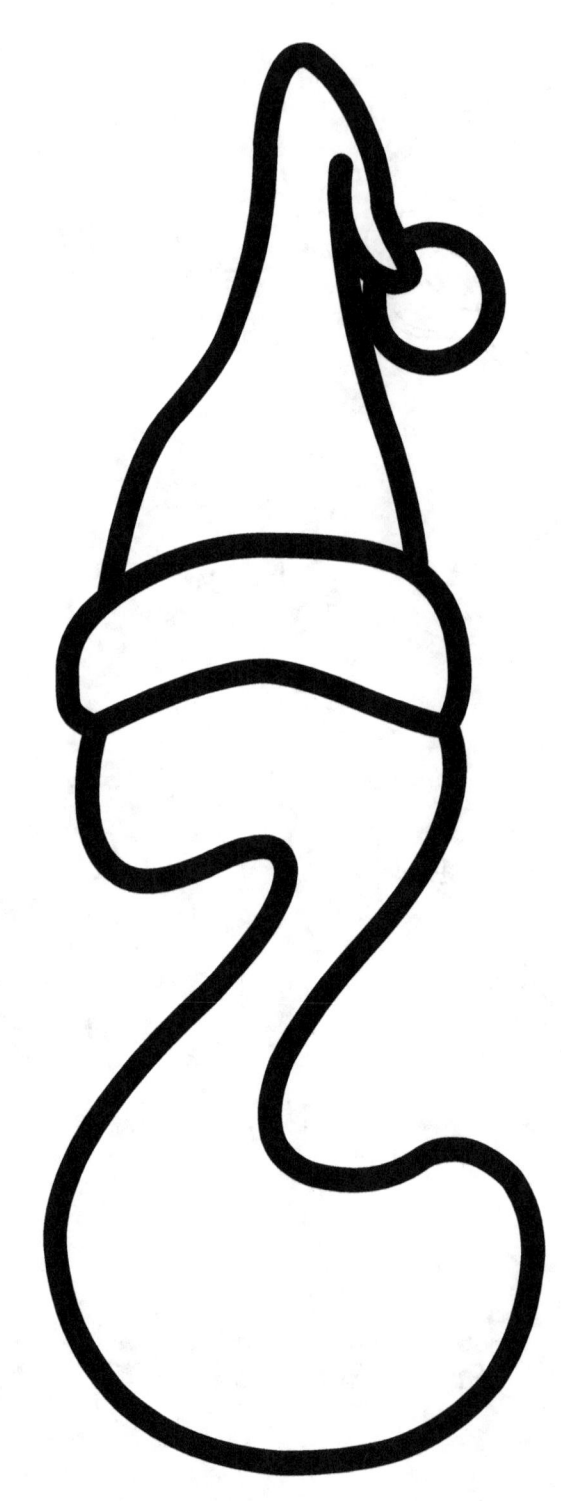

Z z

Thank you for choosing this book!

I hope your child enjoyed the activities in this book, as much we enjoyed creating it.
We are a small family business, so your feedback is very important to us.
If you have encountered any issues with your book, such as printing errors, faulty binding, paper bleeding or any other issue, please do not hesitate to contact us at:

 https://www.facebook.com/LittleEzraPublishing

 littleezra.publishing@gmail.com

Reviews are a brilliant thing for small businesses to grow and improve their quality, so if you enjoyed this book, please consider leaving a review on the website, adding photos of the interior and cover of this book. It takes few minutes, but it would be highly appreciated.

Thank you, again, for choosing us!

www.ingramcontent.com/pod-product-compliance
Lightning Source LLC
LaVergne TN
LVHW060203080526
838202LV00052B/4189